It Happened In Louisiana

It Happened In America Series

It Happened In Louisiana

Remarkable Events That Shaped History

Bonnye Stuart

Globe
Pequot

Guilford, Connecticut
Helena, Montana

Globe
Pequot

An imprint of Rowman & Littlefield

Distributed by NATIONAL BOOK NETWORK

British Library Cataloguing in Publication Information Available

Library of Congress Cataloging-in-Publication Data

Stuart, Bonnye E.
 It happened in Louisiana : remarkable events that shaped history / Bonnye Stuart.
  pages cm — (It happened in America series)
 Includes bibliographical references and index.
 ISBN 978-0-7627-7191-2 (paperback : alkaline paper) — ISBN 978-1-4930-1590-0 (electronic)
 1. Louisiana—History—Anecdotes. I. Title.
 F369.6.S78 2015
 976.3—dc23

                                                        2015022766

∞™ The paper used in this publication meets the minimum requirements of American National Standard for Information Sciences—Permanence of Paper for Printed Library Materials, ANSI/NISO Z39.48-1992.

CONTENTS

CONTENTS

ACKNOWLEDGMENTS

Many thanks go to all those who supported me while researching and writing this book about Louisiana. An earlier trip through the back roads and little-traveled byways of southern Louisiana inspired me to find out more about all the famous and infamous "happenings" in my home state. Many people had so many stories!

I appreciate all the help from the reference librarians at Winthrop University's Dacus Library as well as the encouragement of my peers, especially Marilyn Sarow, who always urges me forward. I feel silly thanking the Internet, but really it is a wonderful resource for writers and history buffs.

Let me also acknowledge my growing and supportive family. Since I wrote *It Happened In New Orleans* our family has grown by leaps and bounds. Our family now includes our children and their spouses: David and Ruby, Elizabeth and Jeff, Jessica Jane and Frank, and Christian and Jessica Lee; and our ten grandchildren Emily, Lauren, Jack, Tennyson, Braden, Lillian, Kingston, Logan, Elle, and Ariadne.

Finally, let me thank my husband, Laurence, who helps me with technical and computer problems, edits my stories at times, and always encourages me to accept whatever challenges come my way.

I hope you enjoy reading these stories about the unique state of Louisiana as much as I enjoyed writing them. I'm sure there are other stories that could have, and should have, made the book, but I did my best to represent the whole of Louisiana and her long and colorful past.

INTRODUCTION

The state of Louisiana was carved out of the 1803 Louisiana Purchase. Her varied history is colored by the diverse nations who ruled over her at various times, sometimes with iron fists, often with laissez-faire attitudes. Her people responded in kind and forged lives uniquely endemic to the area.

Duels in the French tradition continued to preserve a gentleman's honor throughout the 1800s, although they were ruled illegal when Louisiana joined the United States of America in 1812. Disasters were plentiful: Mississippi River logjams, Civil War sieges, boll weevil blights, and the untimely death of the Kingfisher. The last few years brought even more disasters, such as Hurricane Katrina, sinkholes, the disappearance of an entire freshwater lake, and the notorious BP oil spill and its continuing and devastating aftereffects.

Laissez les bon temps rouler! There were good times, too. Towns were settled, oil was discovered, and a historic shipwreck, discovered at the bottom of the Gulf of Mexico, yielded well-preserved artifacts. The record-holding Lake Pontchartrain Causeway has retained its notoriety.

For entertainment, movies were made on location in the swampy marshes and baseball was once king, no matter whether you were black or white. In the 1950s, Elvis ruled the *Louisiana Hayride* and Billy Cannon ran eighty-nine yards to give his beloved LSU Tigers a victory. "The Celebration of Life" rock concert for hippies amused youthful festivalgoers and angered law enforcement officers.

Food, always at the heart of Louisiana life, saw improved varieties of pecans, and that meant even better pies and pralines. Louisiana frogs became part of the regional menu while supplying restaurants around the world. Louisianans loved their animals and gave a Canadian Husky a proper burial and marble monument.

Religion played a huge part in the lives of those who inhabited the region. Catholic saints needing miracles got them. Thousands seeking help from the Virgin Mary prayed for peace in a hot Louisiana field. Lepers searching for a lifelong sanctuary found one on the banks of the Mississippi River.

The call for justice and civil rights was heard on Louisiana soil. From the twenty-five-thousand-strong workers strike of 1892 to Homer Plessey's civil disobedience, men and women fought to right the wrongs against their fellow citizens. Bonnie and Clyde ended their short, murderous lives on a lonely Louisiana road. Other murderers were put to death, a female electrocution made history, and prisoners mutilated themselves to protest the cruelties that occurred behind bars.

In wartime, the Louisiana Maneuvers project trained the leaders of World War II, and Camp Livingston housed its POWs and internees.

Through the years, Louisiana has played its part on the grand stage that is the long and continuous history of our country. Like all skilled actors, its people have the innate ability to rise above the commonplace, a propensity for vivid storytelling, and a unique gift that can take ordinary stories and weave them into an extraordinary tapestry of life. So, it's your turn to play the audience. Grab a piece of pecan pie and a cup of coffee and relax as you enjoy this trip through Louisiana's history.

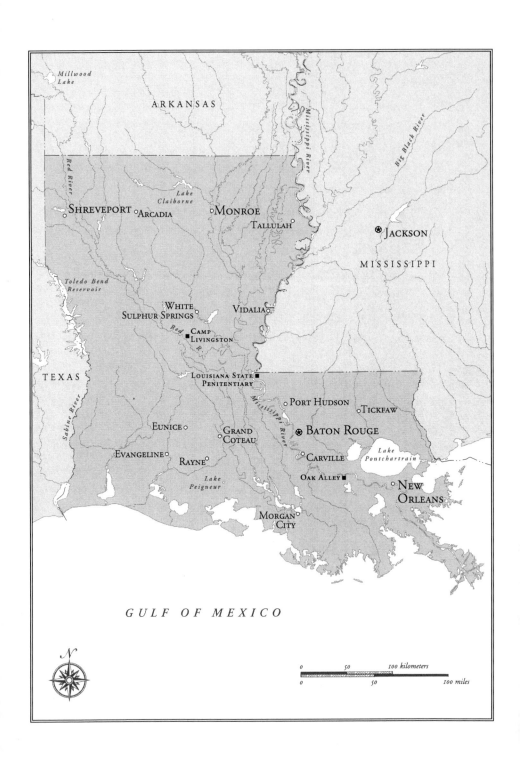

AND SO INTO THE FRAY . . .

1827

In the days when gentlemen settled their disputes by dueling, pistols were a popular weapon of choice. Throughout the first half of the 1800s, dueling was considered the most chivalrous way to confront one's enemy, especially in the French-influenced areas of southern Louisiana. The custom was brought to Louisiana by French settlers who closely guarded their honor and that of their wives and family members.

In the famous Sandbar Duel, however, it was not only a gun that killed participants in the fray that ensued, but also a newfangled nine-inch-blade knife crafted with a guard above the handle to protect the slayer's hand. The Bowie knife, named after its inventor, Jim Bowie, got its fame in Vidalia, Louisiana, and was perhaps first used here in what became known as the Sandbar Duel.

In September 1827, two Rapides Parish men found themselves at odds. It seems Dr. Thomas H. Maddox, a renowned gossiper, had repeated one of his conversations with a lady patient. When pressed for the lady's name, Maddox refused to give it up to General

Montefort Wells. Although two challenges had been declined, a duel was finally set between Maddox and Samuel Levi Wells, a bachelor who would chivalrously take his brother's place, to settle the differences.

The duel quickly escalated into a faction war between longtime rivals with long histories of enmity. Seconds, physicians, and witnesses of family and friends were eager to see justice done.

On one side were Dr. Thomas Harris Maddox, Major Norris Wright, Colonel Robert A. Crain, Alfred Blanchard, Carey Blanchard, Dr. Denny, and other unnamed supporters. The other side consisted of Dr. Samuel L. Wells III, Thomas Jefferson Wells, General Samuel Cuny, James Bowie, George C. McWhorter, and Dr. Richmond E. Cuny.

Wright and Bowie were bitter enemies. Jim Bowie was a notorious adventurer who, along with his brother, Rezin, traded slaves with the infamous Jean Lafitte in New Orleans. He was fit, cunning, and the most feared and respected knife fighter in the South. Norris Wright, although a slight, frail man in appearance, was cool and fearless. He was said to be one of the best pistol shots in the area. In at least two prior duels, he had killed his opponents. The two were on opposite sides of political party squabbles and often competed in land speculation schemes. Wright served on the board of a local bank that had denied loans to Bowie to pay off some land venture debts. Bowie felt Wright was responsible for the refusals. As a further thorn in his side, Wright recently had been named sheriff of Rapides Parish, replacing Sheriff Fristoe, who had been a friend of Bowie's. In one of their altercations, Wright had shot and wounded Bowie. Bowie had managed to pull the gun away from Wright, and some say that if the fight had not been stopped, Bowie would have killed Wright with his bare hands.

Bowie set out for the duel on the sandbar as a friend and supporter of Wells. Because he had had a recent experience with his gun misfiring, he also wore his soon-to-be legendary knife in a silver-mounted black-leather sheath.

Crain and Cuny also had their differences, most of which centered on money and Crain's intent, or not, to pay a bill. Cuny was irate at having to pay off one of Crain's debts because his father was an endorser of the note. Crain was insulted by the accusations dishonoring his name.

The time and place for the duel were set. All parties would meet on September 19 on the first large sandbar above Natchez on the west bank of the Mississippi River. This noted spot for dueling was across the river near Vidalia, Louisiana, a small, sleepy community in Concordia Parish that had been officially established as a town only sixteen years earlier.

The two men brought their seconds, following the "code duello," a 1777 Irish document that contained twenty-six rules for a proper duel, including the time of day, the number of shots allowed for satisfaction, and weapon choice. Duels usually ended with the first drawing of blood. The job of the seconds was to ensure the two men were brought together without premature violence and to attend to the rules.

Both parties were ferried across the river to the large, forested sandbar. The principals, the seconds, and the physicians would be taken to the dueling spot. Friends, supporters, and family members would remain on shore opposite, half a mile away.

Maddox and Wells were gentlemen indeed. The duelists chose their pistols, walked off eight paces, and fired. Both missed. The seconds reloaded the pistols and after two more shots rang out, both men were still standing. The dispute was ended amicably between the two principals. Wells offered an apology, which was accepted by Maddox. The principal duelists resolved their duel with a handshake and started out for a grove of willows to celebrate the new peace with some wine. The duel of honor was complete.

At this time, Bowie and Cuny rushed forward in violation of the agreement to stay put. Cuny called to Crain something about it being a good time to settle their differences; he drew his pistol and shot Crain in the arm. Crain immediately turned and fired his pistols. His bullets hit Bowie in the hip and lung. His shots also mortally wounded General Cuny. Despite his wounds, Bowie reached for the knife he had surreptitiously brought along and charged toward Crain. Crain began hitting Bowie over the head so hard with his empty pistol that Bowie fell to his knees. Wright came to the defense of Crain, drew his pistol, and shot at Bowie on the ground. When the pistol was empty, he and Alfred Blanchard attacked Bowie repeatedly with sword canes, weapons concealed in cane casings typically carried by wealthy men of the period. One thrust hit Bowie in the chest, but the thin blade was deflected by Bowie's thick sternum. Bowie, shot and cut, made a final effort to defeat his enemy. He reached up, grabbed Wright by the shirt, and drew him down toward the knife point. With a sharp twisting plunge of the long-bladed knife, known afterward as the Bowie knife, Bowie fatally stabbed Wright in the heart. Wright died instantly. Bowie, attempting to stand and pull Wright's sword from his chest, was shot and stabbed again by the Blanchard brothers. In the ensuing fray, Bowie managed to cut off part of Alfred's forearm. Carey Blanchard was wounded by a pistol shot from McWhorter.

The melee left Samuel Cuny and Norris Wright dead, and four men, Alfred Blanchard, Carey Blanchard, Robert Crain, and Jim Bowie, seriously wounded. Crain, though in the opposite faction, helped carry Bowie to the doctors. Many believed the fearless Bowie would be dead by morning. He was not. After the Sandbar Fight and subsequent battles in which Bowie displayed his prowess with his knife to defend himself, Bowie figured it was time to get out of town. He sold his land and moved to Texas, married, and raised a family.

When the war between Texas and Mexico broke out, his fate at the Alamo became history.

The Sandbar Fight, called the Vidalia Sandbar Fight locally, is known nationally as the Great Sandbar Duel, thanks to newspaper articles describing the fracas. Rezin P. Bowie was a member of the Louisiana state legislature representing Avoyelles Parish at the time of the duel. He and James owned the Bowie Plantation along Bayou Boeuf, where they cut timber for the lumber industry, farmed, and built homes. Rezin claimed he designed the knife his brother used at the sandbar, as a hunting knife at his plantation. Blacksmith Jesse Clifft, a close friend and neighbor of the Bowies, forged the weapon to resemble a butcher knife, with a nine-inch-long thin blade. Rezin had urged Bowie to take the knife with him to the duel as protection. Eyewitnesses described the "large butcher knife" in personal letters and reporters' interviews. Stories appeared in newspapers across the country, and the legend was born. In a day when pistols frequently misfired, the Bowie knife became a reliable and effective backup weapon. Its popularity spread, and schools were established to teach the art of Bowie knife fighting. The *Red River Herald* of Natchitoches, Louisiana, reported, "All the steel in the country it seemed was immediately converted into Bowie knives." Craftsmen often made their own versions, and by the 1830s, British knife manufacturers were also producing Bowie knives with a standard blade of 8.25 inches long and 1.25 inches wide, and a cross-guard to protect the user's hands.

Dueling died down after the Civil War. Soldiers, tired of war, found bloodshed an unacceptable way to settle their differences. Today, a festival of games, music, and food is held in Vidalia on the fourth Saturday in September to celebrate the event. The 1827 Sandbar Duel reenactment is the highlight of the day.

WHITE SULPHUR SPRINGS: HEALTHY OR HEALTH HAZARD?

1833

The area around Little River, a ninety-six-mile tributary of the Ouachita River and part of the watershed of the mighty Mississippi River, was considered the backwoods of central Louisiana, to be sure! The vital and navigable Little River had trouble keeping a name as settlers moved in and out of the area. The few permanent families called it variously Bayou Des Natchitoches, Catahoula Bayou, Catahoula River, or, more simply and lasting, Little River. Nevertheless, the river provided a much-needed waterway for the logging, fur trading, and cotton transportation industries in the area. As Little River wound its way through the oak-gum bottomland forest dotted with ancient stands of bald cypress, it connected the lush, but isolated, area with the larger world. The Avoyelle, Tunica, Ofo, and Choctaw tribes living here called the watery area "the spring of healing waters." They knew it was a special place. And so did Joseph Ward.

Ward was living in Georgia when his wanderlust kicked in. He had been labeled as an adventurer, and those who knew him best knew he was looking for a new adventure. Ward figured he could find exciting people and places by heading west to Texas. By 1833, he and his fellow travelers were guiding their train of horses across the central plains of Louisiana, looking for a suitable place to camp for the night. When they found a beautiful spring just on the western edge of the Catahoula Prairie District, they decided to stop.

The travelers marveled at the picturesque spot replete with a great variety of trees and shrubs, including the water elm, bitter pecan, cypress, willow oak, and tupelo. Wild fruits and berries and the pungent and aromatic Pepper vine were abundant, along a variety of forbs and grasses. Squirrels, wood ducks, turkeys, deer, rabbit, and woodcock roamed the rural landscape, and excellent fishing was to be had in Little River. Other flora and fauna may have caught Ward's attention. The overcup oak, native to the wetlands, was said to have medicinal properties. Its bark was used to treat fevers, dysentery, bleeding gums, and sore throats; its leaves healed wounds. A concoction of the roots and bark of the Swamp privet, a species of the olive family, provided a healthy beverage, and tea made from the fruit of the mayhaw shrub was a remedy for weak hearts and high blood pressure.

But what really got Ward's attention was the sulfurous liquid bubbling from the springs in the area. The aromatic familiarity reminded him of the home he had left behind, the resort town of White Sulphur Springs, Georgia.

At this time medicinal and restorative resort springs were gaining in popularity. Salt Sulphur Springs, Red Sulphur Springs, Hot Springs, Warm Springs, Bath Alum Springs, Cold Sulphur Springs, Yellow Springs, and Black Springs were being nationally advertised from Tennessee to Ohio and Arkansas to New York as curative spa locations for various ailments.

Dr. J. J. Moorman had expressed the widely held beliefs of the medical profession at the time when he said, "Mineral waters possess great and valuable powers, and are in many cases superior to the medicines of the apothecary's shop; and when used under proper and judicious discrimination, are well qualified to assume a place in the great medical minds of the world." The cures could take many forms: curative, diuretic, sudorific, and alterative. The effects of the mineral-laden waters stimulated glandular secretions, alleviated chronic inflammations, overcame obstructions, and eliminated offensive debris from diseased systems. Patrons who partook of the "waters" were promised that their blood and organs would be restored to their "natural condition." They frequented the mineral water resorts to stimulate languished circulations, revive natural secretions, return elasticity to ailing vessels, and restore energy to muscle and tissue.

Ward decided to settle in the area. To stay connected to his hometown, he named this spot in the Louisiana wilderness White Sulphur Springs and planned to recreate the resort and spa that was so popular in Georgia. He set to work immediately building the resort, as well as the accompanying business establishments the spa would need to succeed. He erected a two-story hotel for overnight patrons and a general merchandise store where guests could get necessities. Ward wanted his resort to be known for its hydropathy, the therapeutic use of mineral water as a cure for all sorts of ailments. For this type of therapy, people would often stay at a resort for months. Some came seasonally; others visited annually. Ward hoped his patrons would enjoy the curative powers of the sulfurous springs so much that they would return often and stay longer.

Of course, attracting a clientele to visit for extended periods of time required offering social entertainment. To indulge his patrons, Ward provided the distractions of a gambling house complete with roulette wheels and card tables, while a spacious dance hall and music accommodated the more lively set. Of course, a place to buy liquor was also needed, so Ward built a welcoming saloon. It is said the

Bowie brothers, Jim and Rezin, who made numerous trips across Louisiana to San Antonio, frequently stopped here. Jim Bowie, often hiding out from creditors (he was involved in a land speculation scheme) and the law (he also engaged in some slave and booty smuggling), found the rural resort a pleasant respite.

As word got out about the luxurious sulfur springs resort, patrons poured into the area. Many traveled by steamboat up and down nearby Little River. LaCroix's Landing became a popular debarkation point. As the "Springs" became a nationally known spa and medicinal resort, Ward built extensive living quarters for his slaves who catered to his guests. Ward was astounded at the success of his resort.

The combination of drinking and bathing procedures produced the best results for sufferers. During the day, ailing patrons drank the bubbling water to cure everything from dyspepsia, jaundice, urinary infections, and diabetes to female diseases, paralysis, bronchitis, and tuberculosis. They also bathed in the medicinal sulfurous springs to ease rheumatism, gout, and diseases of the skin. Freedom from care and rest from weary thought added to the restive atmosphere. As the popularity of the resort grew, so, too, did the rumors. After a story circulated about a local woman discovering a Spanish coin in the dirt bank down along nearby Trout Creek, adventurers flocked to the area. Another popular story was that there were so many fish in Trout Creek, the white perch and trout had to swim upright. The resort became popular for couples looking for a restive spot under the shady trees, as well as invalids looking for the bubbly water that would cure all their ills. Accounts chronicled by a local historian tell tales of so many cured lame patients at the resort that discarded crutches were hauled away by the wagonload. For some guests, simple curative therapies included fishing, walking in the woods, and breathing fresh air.

The "Springs" continued to expand, gaining a nationwide reputation. By 1850, the community had added a grand hotel where champagne-filled glasses were raised in nightly toasts as uniformed slaves doted on guests' every whim. Well-manned livery stables cared for the four-legged visitors. Even the Civil War did not prevent the success of the White Sulphur Springs resort. In fact, stories of wealthy locals who had put their money in wooden kegs and buried them for protection from Union troops brought more fortune seekers to the area after the war. More businesses sprang up as well, indicating that the permanent resident population of White Sulphur Springs was growing. The addition of a cotton mill, gristmill, post office, and schoolhouse firmly established the town's legitimacy. Local families expanded their farm and lumber businesses. Residents took in boarders, opened boardinghouses, and ran hotels. By 1900 the Moffett Hotel, Bethard Hotel, Rollins House, and Whatley House were all in full operation. Catahoula Parish grew so much that it was split to create LaSalle Parish in 1910.

But, times were changing. Modern medical research and practices were gaining in popularity, and hydropathy was declining. In 1911, the Louisiana Board of Health closed the resort down. After an analysis of the sulfurous water, the agency reported that it contained no curative powers and was, in fact, a danger to human health because of the harmful bacteria found in the water. Ward's dream came to an abrupt halt. There is no record to explain Joseph Ward's subsequent sudden disappearance or where he went.

In 1914, a local resident prefabricated a nostalgic octagon pavilion reminiscent of the White Sulphur Springs resort pavilion in the mill yard of Trout Creek Lumber Company. It was transported through the piney hills by team and wagon and erected at the Springs, on Louisiana Highway 8, a few miles southwest of Jena, Louisiana. Today, along with the still-bubbling sulfurous waters, it stands as the only visible evidence of the glory days of Ward's grand dream. In 1982, White Sulphur Springs was listed on the National Register of Historic Places.

BREAKING UP OF THE GREAT RAFT

1835

The pioneers on the small settlement in northern Louisiana eagerly welcomed the renowned Captain Henry Miller Shreve. He was the superintendent of Western River Improvement and a miracle worker. He had already saved towns along the Ohio and Arkansas Rivers. They were hoping he could save their small outpost.

There wasn't much built yet in the area, to be sure, but settlers thought the area had potential. The area sat along the Red River, which, after serving as the boundary line between Oklahoma and Texas, rolls into Louisiana at the northwest corner and flows slowly southeast toward the Atchafalaya and Mississippi Rivers. A small general store had been opened where the Texas Trail crossed the Red River in 1832 by James Huntington Cane and William Smith Bennett. They called the area "Cane's & Bennett's Bluff." Whites were not allowed to settle in this area because it was officially designated as Indian Territory, but they settled anyway. Most itinerants stayed only a season or two to farm the land, grow food, and collect supplies to continue their journey west. But some did remain. The Catfish Hotel was a popular establishment catering to fur traders, cattle rustlers, and river men. Soon saloons, gambling houses, and dance halls appeared on Commerce Street to attract westbound trekkers.

But it was difficult to entice permanent settlers to the young town. Though the town bordered the Red River, navigating it by steamboat was nearly impossible because of huge logjams. The Red carries more silt than any other U.S. river, and its current was extremely slow. A flow less than one mile per hour couldn't dislodge even small snags in the thick, muddy banks. Without an open waterway, supplies brought on the Mississippi River from New Orleans could not reach the settlement. Other rivers had experienced logjams, but the logjam on the Red River was being called the "Great Raft." This raft was an accumulation of centuries of logjams along the river and now spanned over160 miles. The raft was not a continuous run of logs, but rather a series of rafts, frequently broken by large lakes of accumulated water. Water backed up from log rafts on the Red had already created Cross Bayou and Lake Caddo.

Early settlers knew if they wanted a vibrant community, they needed to remove the raft of driftwood and uprooted trees that had been washed from the banks by floods and erosion. These snarls had grown large enough to threaten both the river and its small settlement, but the half-hidden and near-hidden obstructions were great navigational risks to even the most experienced pilots. Some jams were so thick with trees and brush that travelers could ride their horses across the raft and not even realize there was a river underneath. In other places, even the flat-bottomed boats called pirogues used by the local trappers and hunters couldn't snake through.

But when the army had trouble supplying Fort Towson and other posts in the upper Red River Valley and supply convoys were forced to travel the smaller bayous and lakes around the Red River, incurring great expense, something was finally done. The federal government called on Captain Shreve.

The few residents of the settlement anxiously awaited their savior. They had no reason to be optimistic. It was said that the Red River presented the most arduous task of clearing the waterway that the nation had encountered. But they were hopeful indeed. Henry Shreve claimed to have a new method for removing the logs. In February 1833, Shreve arrived in the area under orders from Brigadier General Charles Gratiot, chief of the Engineers of the War Department, to remove the raft. He set up his headquarters in the settlement from which to operate the monumental project. He had less than $25,000 to achieve the miracle everyone was hoping to witness.

On April 11, 1833, Shreve began his five-year task to clear the infamous Great Raft, a 180-mile logjam blocking the Red River. Shreve had brought his newest invention, called a "snag boat." This watercraft was designed with twin hulls, placed eleven or twelve feet apart and connected midship by a huge, but sharp, beam that served as a battering ram. Shreve would drive his boat against each partly submerged tree, ramming it over and over until the entangled mass broke loose. On deck was the "giant claw," a steam-propelled windlass that hauled the trees topside. Next, powerful steam saws would be used to cut the logs into small pieces that were either dumped back into the river to float harmlessly downstream or taken to other sites to build dams.

Shreve began his mission some seventy miles south at the foot of the raft near a settlement called Natchitoches. With 160 men, a supply of dynamite, and his snag boat *Archimedes*, Shreve began his assault on the Red River. By May 5, 1833, they had cleared forty miles.

When Shreve and his crew aboard the *Archimedes* reached the raft near the settlement site, all eyes were glued to the river. They watched as the "snag boat" boat did its work. The shallow-bottomed *Archimedes* took a powerful beating as it rammed the snarl of timber time and time again. Trees as thick as six feet in diameter eventually gave way to its incessant hammering. Other logjam workers stood in the shallow waters, chopping at dense brush and sawing down smaller trees. By the time work stopped in June because of the weather, low water, and pestilence, seventy-one miles had been cleared.

But there was more work to be done. North of the settlement, a huge raft blocked the mouth of Twelvemile Bayou, also called Cross Bayou, where it flowed east from Texas into the Red River in Louisiana. More men and equipment were brought in. By 1835, three hundred laborers were employed in the Great Raft project. Because of the difficult work, the mechanics were paid $10–25 more a month than they had received while working on the Ohio and Mississippi Rivers. Though there were no reported deaths, many workers suffered from extended exposure to the heat, water, and insect bites. Two other snag boats, the *Eradicator* and the *Captain Henry M. Shreve*, were put to work. Unfortunately, the *Archimedes* sunk in November 1836 trying to raise one of the snag boats.

With the success freeing the Red River on the wind, the town fathers worked to build the settlement. In 1835 the Caddo Indians sold their land to the United States, but they saved a 640-acre portion and gave it to the tribe's longtime friend and interpreter, Larkin Edwards. Edwards eventually sold the land to Angus McNeill, James Cane, William Bennett, Thomas Taylor Williamson, Sturgis Sprague, Bushrod Jenkins, James Belton Pickett, and Captain Shreve, a group who had formed The Shreve Town Company to found the town. It was originally named "Shreve's Town" but three years later, on March 20, 1839, it was incorporated and renamed "Shreveport." The sixty-four-city-block community was platted very deliberately, measuring eight blocks west from the Red River and eight blocks south from Cross Bayou; block 23 was the public square. These streets now form present-day downtown Shreveport, the capital of Caddo Parish.

The work of clearing the Great Raft and shoring up the banks of the river and surrounding bayous and lakes was concluded in 1838. The timber that could be salvaged from the Great Raft was taken by barges, steamers, and keelboats, the most notable of which were the *Java*, *Souvenir*, and *Pearl*, to dam up the bayous to prevent runoff water from getting into the main channel of the river.

The lower Red never closed off again due to logjams, turning the region into a lush river delta with scores of rich plantations below Shreveport. New rafts continued to form, blocking the upper reaches of the Red. The Red River, opened by Shreve, remained navigable until 1914 when the railroad replaced the steamboat as the preferred means of transporting goods and people. With disuse the logjams began to form again. In 1986 Henry Miller Shreve became one of the first inductees into the National River Hall of Fame in Dubuque, Iowa, along with Samuel "Mark Twain" Clemens.

PECAN TREES AND GIFTED
SLAVE MAKE HISTORY

1846

Jacques Telesphore Roman, brother of Andre Bienvenu Roman, governor of Louisiana, wanted to do something important like others in his old Louisiana family. He decided to grow pecan trees as a commercial venture, counting on the demand for local pecans to bring income from this additional cash crop to the family coffers. But he needed to find a way to grow trees that produced a higher yield of the nuts. He had purchased the property, now called Oak Alley, a few years earlier in 1836, just two years after his marriage to Marie Therese Celina Josephine Pilie from New Orleans. It was a beautiful site on the bank of the Mississippi River in Vacherie, a few miles upriver from New Orleans and downriver from Baton Rouge. Oak Alley was known for miles around for its double row of twenty-eight stately oak trees, which formed a canopied eight-hundred-foot path leading away from the road. In fact, the legendary oaks were standing before his plantation home was built.

French settlers had planted the oak trees (*Quercus virginiana*) in the early 1700s, and monks traveling through the area in 1722 described the auspicious trees in their journals. The hundred-year-old oaks served as the inspiration for the architecture of the grand plantation home built in 1837–1839 by George Swainy (sometimes Swainey). Roman had been pleased when his father-in-law, Gilbert Joseph Pilie, who loved the beauty of the oak alley, designed a spacious colonnade of twenty-eight large Doric columns to grace all four sides of the mansion.

No corner was cut, and no price was spared, for the construction materials. Bricks were made on the property, and marble was imported from Italy. Special care was taken with the formal gardens and landscaping. As he stood before his magnificent Greek revival–style home of plastered brick, Roman was a proud man.

The mansion had taken two years to build, but the time and expense had been worth it. And although Celina christened the home "Bon Sejour," Pleasant Stay, it continued to be called Oak Alley because of the famed double row of live oaks, fourteen on each side, forming a leafy canopy from the house to River Road, some three hundred yards distant.

To get his new business going, Roman had been trying to graft pecan trees that would yield larger and more abundant pecans. He had heard that planter Amant Bourgeois, just a few miles upriver, had a few good producers on his Anita plantation that yielded nuts with paper-thin shells that made for easier cracking. Roman wanted desperately to grow trees of this type on his property, knowing the thin shell would make harvesting easier and more profitable. The native American pecan tree was very plentiful in the lower Mississippi River basin and along the tributaries that flowed through southern Louisiana and Texas. But the native variety was not a high yielder, and the nuts were small and tough to open. The name came from the Algonquin word "paccan," which referred to all nuts with a hard shell. The French settlers of Louisiana gave the tree its present name, "pecan." The nut of the pecan tree quickly became very popular with early colonists. French settlers in Louisiana substituted pecans for the sweet French almonds when making pralines, the confection so popular in their homeland.

Pecan trees were hard to grow from seeds, and even if they did take root, they were of a low quality. Roman began the first grafting experiments with pecan trees in 1846. But the process was not successful, and the trees would not take the grafts. Eventually he sought outside help and invited Dr. A. E. Colomb, who had also been experimenting with grafting pecan trees, to Oak Alley to carry on his work. Fortunately, Colomb brought some scion cuttings of Amant Bourgeois' high-quality trees with him. Colomb was eager to continue his experiments to graft together two types of pecan trees, but it was an ominous task and one he had failed at before. Many new species of fruits and nuts had been successfully cultivated with the grafting process, but the pecan had stubbornly rejected the process. He needed some help and thought perhaps the locals would know a secret to making the new trees thrive in the local water-soaked plantation soil. He learned that Antoine, one of the field slaves on the Oak Alley Plantation, was well-known for his gardening expertise. Colomb elicited Antoine's help, and the thirty-six-year-old slave became his apprentice. Antoine, one of the 113 slaves on the plantation, loved working with the plants and trees. He carefully took the scions that Colomb had brought to Oak Alley and began the process of grafting them onto the ordinary pecan trees at Oak Alley. Antoine worked diligently; he wanted to succeed for his master, a benevolent slave owner, who had already experienced too many personal tragedies. The plantation was saddened with Celina's loss of several children in infancy and Master Roman's declining health. Roman was considered a benevolent and just master, seeing to it that his slaves were baptized and were given proper church burials. It was Master Roman who had encouraged Antoine in his horticultural work around the plantation.

Antoine was intrigued with the new variety of pecan that Dr. Colomb handed to him. The nut was large and cylindrical and could be cracked open with one hand. The outer crust of the nut was so thin it was referred to as the "paper shell" pecan. And the meat of this pecan was lighter and sweeter than any he had tasted before. He looked forward to the delicacies that could be made with the sweet pecan nut. During that first winter, he tried various techniques to see which grafts would take, working, by trial and error, using the "cleft graft" process. Employing a sharp trimmer, he sliced the scion, the branch from the top-quality producer brought from the Bourgeois plantation, then split a limb from an Oak Alley rootstock. He placed the two cuts meticulously and gently together and sealed the graft with paraffin wax, making one branch of the two pieces.

He was kept busy nursing the young plants, concentrating on keeping alive and healthy the ones that seemed to take. Antoine was a gifted apprentice. By spring, he had successfully grafted sixteen trees. Roman was very happy with the small orchard of grafted trees that Antoine had grown. He had made history as the first planter to grow a commercial orchard with the intention of producing and marketing pecans (*Carya illinoinensis*). But to make pecan harvesting a profitable business, more trees were needed. Antoine was encouraged to continue his work, and by the time Roman died two years later, the slave gardener had successfully grafted 110 trees. This was the first recorded successful effort to graft pecan trees, and it was the first commercial orchard developed to produce nuts for market. Pecans became an important cash crop for southern Louisiana planters and farmers, and the state became known as the cradle of pecan production.

Jacques Roman died of tuberculosis in 1848; he was only forty-eight years old. Celina tried to keep things going with the help of her oldest son, Henri, but the Civil War and its devastating aftermath took its toll on Oak Alley. In 1866, Henri was forced to sell off the plantation at auction for $32,800. But that was not the end for Antoine's modern pecan.

In 1876, part-owner of the plantation, Hubert Bonzano, decided to exhibit the pecans from the Oak Alley grafted trees at the Centennial Exposition in Philadelphia, Pennsylvania. He was proud of the pecan variety and proud to give credit to the accomplishments of the former slave of Jacques Roman, Antoine. The pecans were well received and were awarded a diploma by Prof. William H. Brewer commending their "remarkably large size, tenderness of shell, and very special excellence." The pecan is described as cylindrical, gracefully tapering, bright grayish brown, quite smooth, separating easily from the shell, plump, and solid, with a delicate texture and flavor. It was officially given the name "Centennial" in honor of the hundredth celebration of the birth of the United States, and by 1885 Richard Frotscher's nursery catalogs listed Centennial pecan trees for sale.

Today, two of the original grafted pecan trees still stand on the Oak Alley property and still produce pecans, forty-five to the pound. Serious botanical work with the species continues, and today there are over four hundred varieties of pecan trees that are more productive, yield bigger nuts with thinner shells, taste better, are more resistance to blight, and thrive in specific climate and soil conditions. Unfortunately, the Centennial Pecan, the first pecan cultivar that led to a productive orchard and nursery sales and that represents the beginning of the modern pecan culture, is listed on Gary Paul Nabhan's list of endangered foods.

Oak Alley Plantation—established by its last owner, Josephine Stewart, as a nonprofit foundation—stands fully renovated so that the public can enjoy its beauty and rich past.

LONGEST SIEGE IN U.S.
CIVIL WAR HISTORY

1863

Port Hudson was a small port city situated high on eighty-foot bluffs along the east bank of the Mississippi River where it joined the Red River, just twenty-five miles northwest of Baton Rouge. The town, incorporated in 1832, sat in a sharp hairpin curve of the river. Hills and ridges in an extremely rough terrain of thickly forested ravines and swamps added to the area's isolation. Despite its growing shipping business, Port Hudson consisted of only a few buildings and two hundred people by the start of the Civil War. But Port Hudson would soon make its mark in U.S. history books.

During the Civil War, Port Hudson was vital to the transportation of supplies both east and west and north and south, and the Confederate army was quick to erect batteries that could command the entire river frontage and protect the junction of the Mississippi and Red Rivers. The Union desperately wanted to shut down these supply routes. When New Orleans and Baton Rouge, important Mississippi River ports, fell into Union hands, all eyes turned to Port Hudson.

The soldiers of the Fifteenth Arkansas Infantry Regiment manning the fort were no strangers to war. They had fought at Fort Henry and Fort Donaldson, had been captured at the Confederate surrender, and during seven months in Union prison camps had seen nearly half their comrades succumb to the dire prison conditions. When those still alive were released, the unit was reorganized and stationed at Port Hudson in November of 1862.

In December of 1862, General Nathaniel P. Banks replaced Benjamin Butler as Union commander in the gulf region. Butler's troops remained in New Orleans and when Banks arrived with his own troops, the number of men occupying the Crescent City more than doubled. This troop buildup in Louisiana emphasized Lincoln's commitment to control the Mississippi River. To counter this initiative, Confederate Major General Franklin Gardner was given command of Port Hudson. He immediately began to reorganize the fort, erecting a massive parapet with mounted guns along the bluffs. Exterior trenches running alongside the fortifications made an uphill approach extremely difficult and very dangerous. Soldiers also set up a defense line of packed earth and sod ramparts. Gardner streamlined the supply and storage operations and built protected roads to facilitate the movement of troops.

Port Hudson soldiers awaited the inevitable attack by the Union Army, knowing the battle ahead would be tough. In March 1863, John R. Hardy of the 15th Arkansas Infantry wrote a letter to his family anticipating the coming assault. Although Hardy was confident that the Yankees would not take the fortress at Port Hudson, he talked about the difficult camp life with its many "trials and tribulation." The young man did not know at the time how difficult things would get for him and the rest of the soldiers.

On March 13, just two days after the date on Hardy's letter, U.S. Navy Admiral David Glasgow Farragut was readying his attack fleet of four warships and three gunboats. The vessels were lashed together in an attack column of pairs and their gun decks were whitewashed for better visibility in the nighttime conflict. Huge anchor chains were lashed to the sides of the ships as additional armor.

The Confederate troops, noticing increased naval activity downriver, prepared for the attack. Twenty cannon in eleven batteries were poised. The Rebels had assembled huge stacks of pine wood, which when ignited would illuminate the river for night action. Observation posts set up along the river would fire rockets when enemy vessels approached. The first rocket went off at 11:20 p.m. on March 14. Instantly, shells from battery nine were fired at Farragut's first ship.

The coarse black gun powder produced dense clouds of smoke and when combined with the smoke from the pine wood fires, almost totally obscured the river valley. Blinded by the dense clouds, two of Farragut's ships ran aground on the eastern shore but managed to break free and by 12:15 a.m. had passed out of range of the last Rebel gun position. The rest of the fleet would not be so fortunate. They were hammered by artillery that tore through the ships. Farragut's flotilla was forced to retreat. The soldiers at Port Hudson cheered wildly. However, the two ships that did get past Port Hudson were able to successfully blockade the river. Hardy's letter was probably one of the last from the fort to reach its destination.

Gardner knew that Banks was closing in on Port Hudson by land, as well. Though he wouldn't have Farragut's naval power, Banks was hoping to quickly overrun Port Hudson with his thirty thousand troops. On May 1, 1863, he directed his troops to surround Port Hudson and rout out the enemy. But the seventy-five hundred men at Port Hudson, though outnumbered more than four to one, had other ideas.

The prolonged siege of Port Hudson began with skirmishes on the morning of May 21. By May 22, Union troops had encircled the camp, virtually cutting off all supply routes. Enemy troops continued to advance, but the Confederates held them off. A ferocious battle on May 27 did not go well for the Rebels. Union shelling exploded Confederate guns, killing an officer, wounding the cannoniers, and disabling the guns. The brave men fought on and when Union infantry closed within two hundred yards they were met by a barrage from Rebel forces that included canisters filled with spent bullets, broken chains, pieces of railroad rails, and other scrap iron. The guns equipped to fire this type of ammunition were so effective that Union troops called them the "demoralizers."

Banks resumed his ferocious assaults on June 13, and when he sent a message to Gardner demanding surrender, Gardner replied, "My duty requires me to defend this position, and therefore I decline to surrender." Banks continued the bombardment and ordered a full-out attack on the fort the next morning. But as heavy fog rolled in, Union troops became disoriented in the formidable terrain and the Confederate defense was able to stop the enemy before it neared the fort. At the end of the battle, Union dead and wounded stood at 1,792 compared to the Confederates' 47 causalities.

After this devastation, Union actions against Port Hudson were reduced to bombardment and siege operations, which included fighting from trenches and sharpshooter positions. Sniper fire kept Confederate soldiers at bay while Union troops enhanced their own trench lines and disabled enemy batteries.

The Confederates responded to the siege techniques with increased efforts of their own. Additional trench lines, mines, bunkers, telegraph wire booby traps, and other obstacles made the fort more difficult to overrun. On June 26, the Confederates, using improvised hand grenades, captured Union prisoners, weapons, and supplies. Other raids struck at Union foraging parties, set fire to a

Union supply center, and exploded a Union mine. These efforts did not break the siege.

Inside the fort, conditions were deteriorating. Men existing on corn bread and syrup were weak and near starvation. Mule, dog, and rat meat could not sustain the soldiers, who succumbed to scurvy and dysentery. Those who didn't suffer from sunstroke, fatigue, ague, fevers, and, worse, malaria, were the first to fall from sniper shots and enemy shelling. Soldiers who could still load and fire a gun continued the battle against the larger and better-supplied Union troops. The enemy advanced again and again, eventually coming within forty yards of the encampment. The desperate fighting of desperate men managed to hold them off. The soldiers, knowing the perilous situation they were in, began to refer to the camp as "Fort Desperate."

Even though artillery barrages and sniper fire threatened the fort day after day, the Confederates continued to hold firm. The Union was stunned by the decisive defeats of their infantry assaults, but Banks was determined to continue the siege, knowing that his political and military career would be over if he withdrew. The resources of his entire command were brought into play, and men from nine additional regiments came to the aid of the Union.

Despite the hardships of the hopeless situation, the Port Hudson section of the Confederate line was never breached by Union forces. But on July 9, 1863, after hearing of the fall of Vicksburg, which gave Union ships access to the Mississippi and Red Rivers, Confederate General Gardner at Port Hudson surrendered. There was no reason to hold out any longer. The Mississippi River was now in the hands of the Union, and the Confederacy was divided in half.

The battle of Port Hudson was costly to the Union Navy and Army, which saw its highest casualty numbers of the Civil War there. A significant result of the siege was the blow it gave Banks's political career. If he had taken Port Hudson in May, he could have taken command of Grant's siege of Vicksburg as the ranking officer, but since Vicksburg fell before Port Hudson, Grant was awarded the victory, and eventually attained the White House, Banks' cherished ambition.

The Port Hudson State Commemorative Area sits on the northern portion of the battlefield where four thousand Civil War veterans are buried at Port Hudson National Cemetery. Remnants of Fort Desperate are overgrown with brush, but earthen works and trenches are still identifiable. The park is open from 9:00 a.m. to 5:00 p.m. daily.

HE NEEDED ANOTHER MIRACLE

1866

Grand Coteau, an unassuming town in St. Landry Parish, has made the annals of history a few times. At one time the region is believed to have hugged the west bank of the Mississippi River, thus its name Grand Coteau, meaning "big hillside," referred to the area along the sloped levee of the river. But today the area is nearly sixty miles from the river. In 1776 the area was part of the first known land grant, Prairie ses Femmes, from the Louisiana colonial government. In 1821, the wealthy widow of planter Charles Smith invited Sister Rose Philippine Duchesne, a Sacred Heart nun from Grenoble, France, who was establishing schools throughout Louisiana, to Grand Coteau. Smith donated four hundred arpents of land and a two-story building to the order of nuns. Duchesne was canonized in 1988 by Pope John Paul II. The Sacred Heart Academy is the second oldest learning institution west of the Mississippi River. During the Civil War's "Campaign of the Teche," the area saw several skirmishes and the 1863 Battle of Grand Coteau resulted in a Confederate victory, but the convent and school of the Sacred Heart was untouched.

Union General Nathaniel Banks had a daughter in a school run by the Sacred Heart Order in New York, who asked him to keep the sisters and students in Grand Coteau safe. He did.

In 1866, the religious environment of the area again made history. Canadian Mary Wilson was a Sacred Heart postulant in poor health. She was sent to the order's convent in the mild climate of Grand Coteau, Louisiana, in hopes that her health would improve. She arrived on September 20, 1866, and was to take her final vows and receive her habit a month later. Her health continued to deteriorate. She was dangerously ill and vomited up blood two or three times a day. On October 19, twenty-year-old Mary was confined to the convent's infirmary. Though this was a quiet sanctuary for the ailing young religious, her condition did not improve. She suffered from severe headaches and constant fever. She spoke of a sharp pain in her side. Mary could eat nothing, though she managed to sip a little coffee and tea. The pain was excruciating, and her hands and feet were drawn up in debilitating cramps. Her skin felt cold as death. Her stomach and throat were inflamed. She could no longer speak due to a raw and swollen tongue. When she attempted to form words, blood spurted from her mouth. Even keeping medicine down was impossible, and soon the medication was stopped. The doctor said it was useless to torture the young woman any further. After nearly forty days without food, and the last two days without even water, she was left to die.

Mary was not finished with life, however. Mary's heart reached out to God in an unspoken prayer, "Lord, Thou Who seest how I suffer, if it be for your honor and glory and the salvation of my soul, I ask through the intercession of Blessed Berchmans a little relief and health. Otherwise give me the patience to the end. I am resigned." The sisters of the Sacred Heart also began to pray for their dear Mary in the name of John Berchmans, a Belgian Jesuit who had been declared blessed by Pope Pius IX in 1865, the step before being named a saint. Berchmans was devoutly religious, and he died in Rome at the age of twenty-two. He, too, had been confined to an infirmary where his fever ran rampant and his lungs became inflamed. He had been credited with many miracles on his road to beatification, but the Catholic Church required three more miracles for canonization, and he only had two. He was in need of a third miracle.

For days the nuns held a prayer card with Berchmans' image in front of the dying novice, beseeching his help to cure the ailing nun who was so close to taking her sacred vows. But to no avail. The young girl was given the last rites, and the end was thought to be very near. One day one of the sisters placed the prayer card on Mary's mouth and instructed Mary to keep praying. Mary spoke silently to Blessed John Berchmans, "If it be true that you can work miracles, I wish you would do something for me." The young novice heard a voice whisper to her, "Open your mouth." Painfully, the girl did as she was told. She felt someone put a finger on her tongue and almost immediately she felt relief of the inflammation that had reigned in her mouth. Then she hear the voice again, saying, "Sister, you will get the desired habit. Be faithful. Have confidence." The voice continued, "Fear not."

When Mary opened her eyes, she saw a man's figure standing by her bed. In his hands was a cup. Mary was afraid and closed her eyes tight once again. She asked the visitor, "Is it Blessed Berchmans?" The apparition answered, "Yes, I come by order of God. Your sufferings are over." Once again he advised her, "Fear not."

When Dr. Millard called in at the infirmary that evening to check on his patient, he was astonished to see the young woman greet him at the door. He was overcome with surprise and nearly fainted. The doctor examined Mary's mouth and tongue and was shocked to see that all was healed.

Mary's strength returned immediately, and her body healed quickly. Her suffering was over. She began to eat and drink. She returned to a healthy mind and body and continued her duties of community life. She said later in her detailed account of the ordeal, "For the glory of Blessed John Berchmans, whose name be ever blessed! I deem it my duty to declare here, that from the moment of the cure I never experienced the slightest return of my former ailments."

Dr. Millard's sworn statement, made on February 4, 1867, attests, "Not being able to discover any marks of convalescence, but an immediate return to health from a most severe and painful illness, I am unable to explain the transition by any ordinary laws."

About eight months later, John Berchmans appeared to Mary again, saying, "I'm taking you to God." Shortly thereafter, Sister Mary died. Her grave lies in the small Sacred Heart cemetery just behind the academy, inscribed with the word "miracle."

Many miracles had been attributed to John Berchmans, from curing blindness to healing the sick. The process of sainthood is long and arduous. The last miracle needed by John Berchmans to be sainted by Pope Leo XIII in 1888 was that of his visitation and cure of Mary Wilson. The similarity between the modest, unassuming young people involved in this story who were united in sanctity, even though separated by centuries and continents, is not unnoticed.

The miracle of Grand Coteau is part of Roman Catholic Church history. The official prayer to St. John Berchmans reads, "John, our brother, you already enjoy the face-to-face vision of God. Please remember us to Him as we struggle here on earth to attain the joy you now possess." Today a simple chapel sits on the holy site where the miracle in the infirmary took place. It is the only shrine in the United States at the exact location of a miracle confirmed by the Catholic Church.

TWENTY-FIVE THOUSAND
WORKERS UNITE

1892

By 1890, New Orleans was the second busiest port in the country after New York City. Agricultural products, lumber and other raw materials, coal, and the southern cash crops of sugar, rice, and cotton flowed through the city's river and railroad networks, gateways to other parts of the world. The need for swift, cheap, and dependable manufacturing and transportation often meant worker exploitation by employers who wanted to increase profits. It was perhaps inevitable that the workers, white and black laboring side by side, would form alliances and join labor unions that were growing in power, to better their bargaining position despite the intense opposition of employers and government.

Early in 1892, streetcar conductors in New Orleans had won unprecedented gains and were enjoying a shorter work week and a closed labor union shop, which protected workers from belligerent employers and arbitrary hiring and firing practices. This victory of workers over rich and influential bosses spurred a frenzy of union organization around the city. By the late summer of 1892, more than forty labor unions had joined the American Federation of Labor (AFL) and were organized under a central organization called the Workingmen's Amalgamated Council representing more than twenty thousand workers seeking better wages and conditions. The Teamsters, the Scalesmen, and the Packers became known as the "Triple Alliance," and they made their demands of a ten-hour workday, overtime pay, and a preferential union shop (an agreement in which an employer must consult the union when hiring new employees) to unreceptive management.

By early fall things had reached a feverish pitch and on October 24, between two and three thousand union members of the Triple Alliance went out on strike.

Immediately, employers of the financial and commercial interests in the city, including the shipping industry, the four railroads serving the area, and the large cotton, rice, and sugar exchanges, banded together under the New Orleans Board of Trade. The Board began to raise money for a defense fund for big business and its efforts to break the strike. It thought its best strategy for success against a strike was to divide the workers and garner public support for their cause by appealing to racist prejudices. The Board announced it would sign new contracts, but only with the white-dominated Scalesmen and Packers unions. Bosses feared that the black-dominated Teamsters would gain too much power over white employers if they won any of their demands.

When the divide-and-conquer tactic didn't work, the Board elicited the cooperation of the city's bigoted newspapers, which began a campaign to portray black unionists as "mobs of brutal Negro strikers" taking to the streets "beating up all who attempted to interfere with them." Between the emotion-arousing articles about the lurid behavior of strikers and the Board's predictions of a reversal in power, public hysteria ensued.

But the Alliance held firm. Well-disciplined strikers maintained orderly, nonviolent picket lines. They refused to break along racial lines.

The prolonged and arrogant refusal of the New Orleans Board of Trade to negotiate seriously with three unions sparked allegiance from fellow workers. Soon other unions began to call for strikes to support the Triple Alliance. Meetings were called and votes were tallied. A Committee of Five was formed of the Screwman's Union, the Cotton Yardman's Union, the Printers Union, the Boiler Makers Union, and the Car Driver's Union. This Committee of Five would lead the scheduled mass walkouts.

The possibility that all these unions, including the organized hatters, the shoe clerks, and musicians, would strike encouraged smaller employers to appeal to the Board of Trade to negotiate with the unions. But it was all to no avail.

The "general strike call" was issued on November 8, 1892, and just as they had threatened, all member unions of the Amalgamated Council went out on strike, from the recently organized utility workers to the longer-established Teamsters. The twenty-five to thirty thousand strikers comprised almost half the city's workforce. While even some unorganized workers joined the action, streetcar drivers and printers, in violation of their contracts, joined the general strike.

"Tie the town up!" was the battle cry of strikers. And they did. Streetcars stopped moving along the busy thoroughfares and retail clerks and office workers could not get to their jobs in the city. Food and beverage delivery was halted, leaving stores with little or no inventory. Streets were left unclean, manufacturing plants ground to a halt, and construction projects were stilled. The city's electrical grid collapsed, plunging the city into darkness for three nights; firefighting services were unavailable; and the natural gas company stopped the flow of gas into homes and businesses. Businesses in the city were virtually paralyzed, but worse, city residents were in a state of panic and terror.

On November 9, the *New Orleans Times-Democrat* intensified its appeals to racial hatred, reporting that black men sought to "take over the city" and that white women and children were being harassed by black strikers. Again, these bogus accounts failed to deter the strikers. They held fast, determined to build a reputation of cooperation and alliance that crossed color lines. Strikers were encouraged by union leadership to stay the course, and even though the daily newspapers were replete with scare tactics, New Orleans residents could observe for themselves that although the city was at a commercial standstill, it remained peaceful and calm. All the while, special agents of the Board roaming the streets anxiously looking for any outbursts of violence found none. Picket lines were quiet, and no violent incidents were ever documented.

Strikebreakers from as far away as Galveston, Texas, and Memphis, Tennessee, were called up and transported to the city by railroad companies that supported the big business holdout. The mayor of New Orleans, who supported the workers, called for volunteer deputies to handle the strikers. When only a small number of recruits stepped up, employers began to train their own company clerks and managers as a private militia. They demanded the governor send in the military to help contain the strikers. Louisiana Governor Murphy J. Foster, a known racist, threatened to declare martial law and forbid the gathering of crowds. On November 10, he sent several battalions of the state militia into the city. But when they found a city calm and orderly, the governor was forced to rescind the order and the militia was withdrawn the very next day, but not without threats to send in five thousand militia troops to break up the picket lines if the strike was not settled.

Finally, the Board of Trade, concerned with reports that banking activity had dropped below 50 percent of its pre-strike levels, and the unions, fearing confrontation with the threatened five-thousand-man militia, consented to submit to binding arbitration to settle the strike. The Board was forced to sit down to face-to-face meetings with both white and black union leaders in grueling negotiations that lasted forty-eight hours. Compromise was found on both sides of the table. Employers had little choice but to agree to the ten-hour workday, overtime compensation after sixty hours, and a 25 percent wage increase. But, and this was a big "but," they did not agree to the union shop or union recognition. Strikers had won some concessions but had lost their most important demand—the closed shop.

The Board of Trade, deeply angered with being brought to its knees by the general strike, filed a suit in federal court against forty-four of the unions and sought indictments against forty-five strike leaders, accusing them of violating the Sherman Antitrust Act. A district court granted a temporary injunction against the unions, a moot point because the workers were already back at work. The AFL appealed the suit. The injunction was stayed and the case was delayed in court for several years, eventually being withdrawn by the federal government.

The 1892 general strike strengthened the labor movement in New Orleans and the unions increased in membership. The success of the strike demonstrated that black and white workers could come together for a mutual cause. The strikers had avoided violence, won most of their demands, avoided military repression, and succeeded in overcoming racial hatred. Samuel Gompers, founder and president of the AFL, said, "To me the movement in New Orleans was a very bright ray of hope for the future of organized labor." However, others declared the massive strike a failure, accusing unions of "selling out" their demands for a union shop. Soon after the strike, the Amalgamated Council collapsed and in the face of the 1893 economic depression, the rising tide of white supremacy eroded the gains that had been made in race relationships. Nevertheless, historians have applauded the 1892 strike's significance in overcoming racial divisions among black and white, skilled and unskilled, laborers in the Deep South, a solidarity that would rarely be seen again until the 1960s.

MAN BOARDS THE "WRONG" RAILCAR

1892

In 1892, thirty-year-old Homer Adolph Plessey was enjoying a pretty successful life. He had followed in his shoemaker stepfather's shoes, so to speak. He was employed by Patricio Brito's shoe-making company on Dumaine Street just outside the French Quarter. He married the lovely Louise Bordenave and had time and energy to be active in social causes. He served as vice president of the Justice, Protective, Educational, and Social Club, an organization committed to educational reform in the city. Homer had been born Homère Patrice Plessy, but his birth certificate had been later changed and his father's middle name of Adolph appeared behind the Americanized "Homer." His Plessy grandfather had been a white Frenchman who arrived in New Orleans from Haiti during the slave rebellion of the 1790s. His grandmother had been a free woman of color, Catherine Mathieu. Plessy grew up speaking French in his mixed-race household.

The black community of New Orleans, infused with French, Island, African, and American nuances, was a forceful leader in the fight against segregation. Its members were people of culture, business, education, professionalism, and some wealth, and they had important connections throughout the city. They had also enjoyed their freedom for several generations. Activists Rodolphe Desdunes and Louis Andre Martinet helped start a local chapter of the American Citizens Equal Rights Association (ACERA), a national civil rights group. When a law requiring separate railcars for blacks and whites was introduced in the Louisiana legislature, New Orleans citizens organized to fight it. A delegation of ACERA addressed the Louisiana Legislature, but little came of the confrontation. Many members felt powerless, and disquieting intimidation by whites resulted in weakening the organization. The legislature passed Act 111 of 1890 ("The Separate Car Act"), which segregated railroad passenger cars for the first time.

The black community was not to lie down quietly. On September 1, 1891, a group of eighteen prominent "men of color" formed the Comité des Citoyens (Committee of Citizens) and committed this organization to the repeal of the railcar law. Martinet, attorney and publisher of *The Crusader* newspaper, and attorneys Albion Tourgee and James C. Walker handled the legal strategy. Aristide Mary, a wealthy Creole, would provide critical funding for the upcoming legal battles. Desdunes wrote inspirational pieces and enthusiastic editorials as editor of *The Crusader*, a weekly black newspaper, printed in French and English, which informed and rallied the community to challenge the encroaching segregationist laws. Meetings of the Comité des Citoyens were held at the newspaper's offices.

In February 1892, the group staged its first public demonstration challenging "The Separate Car Act." Rodolphe Desdunes' son, Daniel, bought a ticket for Mobile, Alabama, and boarded the Louisville & Nashville Railroad. He sat in a white coach and refused to move. All went according to plan. Desdunes was arrested, released on bail, and a trial was set. In Desdunes' case, the court determined that if a passenger was traveling between states, then the federal law for equality held true. Desdunes was acquitted, so as an interstate passenger his challenge did nothing to change either Louisiana law or its practice. Black folks were still being required to sit in separate train cars in Louisiana. Four months later another Creole, Homer Plessy, stepped up to challenge the law by traveling solely within Louisiana.

Because of his one-eighth of African descent, Plessy was considered an "octoroon" by society and although he had light skin, he was classified as "black." This meant he would have to suffer the infringement of many civil rights, including being forced to sit in the "colored" car of the railroad line.

Plessy was a member of the Comité des Citoyens, younger than many of the politicians, attorneys, businessmen, and literary minds who were his fellow members. But Plessy had a strong mind and was determined to make a difference. He was ready to test the constitutionality of the Louisiana separate car law.

The East Louisiana Railroad Co. had thirty-six miles of rails in the state and was offering excursions to the "Great Abita Springs" for only a dollar. On Tuesday evening, June 7, 1892, though he knew he would not be visiting the springs that day, Plessy bought a first-class ticket to the small village of Covington at the Press Street Depot in downtown New Orleans.

With ticket in hand, Plessy walked confidently to the "whites only" car of the East Louisiana Railroad and, in a proud act of civil disobedience, boarded. He was aware that he could be arrested for violating the Separate Car Act. In fact, this was exactly the plan, and to ensure Plessy's detainment, the Committee hired a private detective with the power to arrest to be on the scene.

As Plessy sat anxiously in his seat in the "whites only" railcar, he thought about his stand on this issue. His light skin often was mistaken for white, and though he could get away with breaking some laws, he knew it was the principle of the segregation as a lifestyle that irked him. The committee hoped Plessy's lighter skin would not only draw white people's sympathy to his plight but also demonstrate that laws based on skin color were arbitrary. The railroad, a willing player in this challenge, not wanting the expense of providing separate, often less than full, cars, had been previously notified of Plessy's status as a black man. His sitting in the white car, though he might have "passed," needed to be questioned.

The train started up and began to move slowly down the tracks. Plessy adjusted a little in his seat. Soon the railroad conductor, J. J. Dowling, entered the car and approached down the aisle, ticket-puncher in hand. When he stood before Plessy, Dowling asked, "Are you a colored man?" Plessy responded he was. He was told to immediately vacate his seat and sit instead in the blacks-only car. Plessy refused to move. When Private Detective Chris C. Cain told Plessey he would be arrested if he did not change cars, Plessy replied that he "would sooner go to jail than leave the coach." On hearing this admission, he was arrested. The train was stopped and Plessy was taken off at Press and Royal Streets. Plessy was taken to the Orleans Parish jail. He was released the next day on a $500 bond and a trial date would be set. Plessy had fulfilled his mission: buy a ticket, board the train, and get arrested. The *Daily Picayune* newspaper ran an article two days later with the double headline, "Another Jim Crow Car Case. Arrest of a Negro Traveler Who Persisted in Riding With the White People."

Plessy began a historical journey that day in 1892. On his court date he came up against Judge John Howard Ferguson, a Massachusetts-born teacher-turned-attorney who had moved to New Orleans in 1865. Ferguson lived in uptown New Orleans with his wife, Virginia, and three growing sons. He had come up the judicial ranks, practicing law in the city until he became a judge of the criminal district court where he would preside over Plessy's case. First his case was tried in the Louisiana courts. In *Homer Adolph Plessy v. The State of Louisiana*, Judge John Howard Ferguson ruled that providing separate railcars for blacks and whites was not covered by the Thirteenth and Fourteenth Amendments of the U.S. Constitution, as argued by Plessy's attorneys, because travel within a state fell under a state's constitutional right to set railroad regulations within their borders. Plessy was convicted and fined $25. The Comité des Citoyens appealed Plessy's case to the Supreme Court of Louisiana, which upheld Ferguson's ruling. Next stop was the U.S. Supreme Court, which decided to hear the case, now designated *Plessy v. Ferguson*. The case, finally tried in 1896, resulted in a seven-to-one decision rejecting Plessy's attorneys' arguments and contending that separating the two races did not indicate inferiority. Finding no difference in the quality of accommodations for the different railcars, this landmark Supreme Court ruling cemented the legal foundation for the "separate but equal" doctrine that would last until its repudiation in1954 in the Supreme Court decision *Brown v. Board of Education*. The lone dissenter, Justice John Marshall Harlan, used wording from the Comité des Citoyens original filings for his "Great Dissent" paper, writing that "we shall enter upon an era of constitutional law, when the rights of freedom and American citizenship cannot receive from the nation that efficient protection which heretofore was unhesitatingly accorded to slavery and the rights of the master." Plessy's short ride on the tracks of New Orleans had made history.

In January 1897, Homer Plessy pled guilty to violating the law, paid his fine, and dedicated his time to religious and social activities. He eventually gave up the shoe-making business and sold insurance for People's Life Insurance Company in New Orleans. He died in 1925 and rests in an aboveground tomb in St. Louis Cemetery #1, upon which a plaque outlines his role in history. A sign stands at the corner of Press and Royal Streets, near the location of the former railway station where Plessy boarded the train, commemorating his actions on June 7, 1892, violating the Louisiana 1890 Separate Car Act.

THE HOME THAT FEAR BUILT

1894

The small group huddled together waiting to board the coal barge being towed along the Mississippi River bank to the wharf by the sturdy tugboat. The old warehouse where they stood was dark and musty. It was the dead of night and they were scared. What lay ahead for them in the strange new place upriver?

Though some gentle caregivers, such as the beloved Father Damien, chaplain at Charity Hospital, had been kind to their lot, others were cruel. When he contracted the unmentionable disease and died in 1882, it was only a matter of time before they were outcasts from society. They were uncertain what the future held for them, but they knew this was the best course of action.

Dr. Isadore Dyer, a physician at the Tulane University Medical School in New Orleans, was with them and tried to ease their fears. He had a special interest in their disease and wanted only the best of care for them. He had tried to secure a place for them in New Orleans but had met resistance from the fearful citizenry at every turn. Finally, Mr. Allen Jumel, a member of the Louisiana House of

Representatives, managed to negotiate, under the guise of starting an ostrich farm, a five-year lease on some abandoned property outside the city along the river. He told the group that their new home was in an area called Carville, named after Louis Arthur Carville, the postmaster. Carville was part of the town of St. Gabriel in Iberville Parish, sixteen miles south of Baton Rouge. Here they would live and be cared for on Indian Camp Plantation, an antebellum sugar plantation built around 1857 by Robert Coleman Camp. He had given the home its name because it was said the property had once been a Houma Indian village. Dr. Dyer tried to prepare the voyagers for the condition of the once-elegant plantation home, which had fallen into decay during the Civil War when the Camps lost their fortune. The plantation had been sold at a sheriff's auction in 1874 to Henry J. Budington of New Orleans and now sat unclaimed by his heirs in France.

On this night Dr. Dyer was also transporting a huge load of medical supplies, bedding, and eighty beds furnished by Charity Hospital in New Orleans. He had big plans for the facility, both in caring for patients and in finding a cure for the awful disease.

It was November 30, 1894, and the patients were victims of the dreaded disease leprosy (now called Hansen's disease after Gerhard A. Hansen, who first identified the microbe in 1874). At this time southern Louisiana was reporting some of the highest numbers of people afflicted with leprosy in the country. It was thought that the disease had been brought over by two groups: early European settlers and fleeing Acadians from Canada's Maritime Provinces who were seeking refuge in Louisiana. The French-speaking Cajuns and Creoles of southern Louisiana called the disease *la maladie que tu nommes pas*, or "the illness you do not talk about." But by the late 1700s, the disease had seemed under control. Unfortunately there was a reappearance of the disease in the mid-1800s throughout the Southwest, probably brought by immigrants from the West Indies. New fears began to arise among the population as more and more cases were reported. Contagion was the issue; many wanted the afflicted persons quarantined and out of sight. The future was very bleak for those who contracted the disease. The scourge of having leprosy was so acute that traveling anonymously in the middle of the night was the only alternative for public transportation and the deserted plantation was the only available housing option.

The trip up the river was eerie and disquieting, but the barge finally pulled up along the levee in an isolated bend in the Mississippi River just south of Baton Rouge. The group disembarked quietly and hurriedly, scampered over the high levee and across the desolate River Road, and entered the sprawling grounds of the 395-acre Indian Camp Plantation. They found their way to the once beautiful, two-story main house and could see right off that it was in bad need of repairs; it was vermin-infested and in no condition to accept patients. Until it was cleaned and renovated, they would stay in the seven dingy slave quarters still standing on the property.

The November night had turned into December dawn and hopes were high for the new place of refuge and healing. Local physician Dr. L. A. Wailes would see to their immediate medical needs, but they would need to band together and take good care of themselves. The patients looked wide-eyed around the plantation grounds. The ancient, gnarled oak, twisting and turning upon itself, caught their eyes and seemed to epitomize the ravages of the monstrous disease on the human body, but the two magnificent live oaks with thick lacy clumps of Spanish moss on another part of the property were more uplifting symbols of their new start. They seemed to denote vibrancy and long life. The property was fenced to keep patients in—and visitors out. The new residents were given identification numbers and were allowed to choose their own fictitious names. This practice would continue. A person's real identity could be found only in the hospital's legal legers; even grave markers were engraved with the deceased's number and "new" name.

Day-to-day life was hard, but the patients began to make a home for themselves. They cleared and cleaned, walked when they could, fished in Carville's lake, and helped each other with small tasks. They had left family and friends behind along with their identities. They knew they would never return to their previous lives and were determined to mark the positive milestones. They began to plan Mardi Gras celebrations in the new year. Perhaps they could decorate their wheelchairs as carnival floats. They knew the future of the hospital depended on them establishing a viable community at Carville, and they really wanted the colony to succeed.

Unfortunately, after only a year Dr. Wailes left the institution and the patients' health suffered, supplies often ran low, and there was a problem with the water. But by 1896, things were looking up for the residents, who now numbered thirty-one. In late March, Dr. Dyer had journeyed to Maryland and contracted with Mother Mariana of the Daughters of Charity of St. Vincent de Paul for four Catholic nuns to live at Carville and care for the patients. They arrived on April 27, 1896, under the leadership of Sister Beatrice Hart, and assumed control of the leprosarium, running the infirmary and patients' living quarters. They acted as nurses, therapists, pharmacists, researchers, and even dieticians. Other responsibilities included administrative duties, maintenance work, research, and political advocacy for the hospital. They would work at the Carville Leper Home, as it was originally called, for over a hundred years. A local chapter of the religious order was inaugurated, and a priest was assigned to take care of the sisters' spiritual needs. The Daughters of Charity lived in a two-story house facing River Road. They rose at 4:00 a.m., attended mass, and then began taking care of their patients.

The nuns took vows of charity, poverty, obedience, and service to the poor. As employees of the U.S. Public Health Service, they received an expense allotment of $100 a year, which they donated to charity.

In just under two years, the experiment of Carville had succeeded. Leprosy victims had a place to call their own. They began to set up the necessary infrastructure for a small village, opening a store, post office, theater, and recreation hall. They started fund-raising for a new church and began publishing their own magazine, *The Sixty-Six Star*. But isolation still reigned.

In 1905 the state purchased the site, making the leprosarium a permanent institution. On February 3, 1917, a bill was enacted to acquire the site as a national leprosarium, but the action was delayed because of World War I. On January 3, 1921, after the war was over, the leprosarium was purchased by the U.S. government and became the U.S. Public Health Service Marine Hospital No. 66. The U.S. flag was raised February 1.

Patients were legally quarantined at Carville until the 1960s.

In 1984 the Carville leprosarium became the Gillis W. Long National Hansen's Disease Center. Today leprosy is completely curable using multidrug therapy (MDT). Worldwide, the disease has decreased 90 percent since 1985. Carville closed its doors in 1999.

For over one hundred years, more than five thousand leprosy patients were cared for at Carville; some one thousand are buried on the property. Each tombstone is inscribed with a number, fictitious name, and the true date of birth and death of the person. Carville is on the National Registry of Historic Places. The National Hansen's Disease Museum is located at 5445 Point Clair Road. The museum is open to the public, free of charge, Tuesday through Saturday, from 10:00 a.m. to 4:00 p.m. Carville was used by thousands of National Guard troops and public health officials assisting with relief efforts after Hurricane Katrina.

BIGGEST AUCTION IN TOWN

1895

Prairie Faquetaique was just a speck on the rural Louisiana landscape, but C. C. Duson saw potential. He had moved to the small community of a lone general store and a few modest homes after purchasing a significant tract of property from Willie Humble. However, Duson was not happy with the slow growth of the area; he wanted his new home to flourish quickly. He had already founded the town of Crowley (1887) twenty miles to the south, with his brother W. W. Duson, and he wanted another feather in his cap. His first wife had died, leaving him with eight children, and now he had a new wife and an infant son, Curley. Another son would be on the way soon. Duson was poised for a bright future, and he had a plan to make it happen.

His plan was this: He subdivided 160 acres of his Prairie Faquetaique land into 50-by-140-foot residential lots, twelve lots to a block. The few people in the area were intrigued by Duson's work to map out a town site as he laid out the wide east-west streets and north-south intersecting roads on either side of a central boulevard. While the town plat was being drawn and laid out, Duson persuaded the

Southern Pacific Railroad to extend a branch line north from Crowley to the new town. Then he began his land promotion campaign. The kicker of this plan was that he would hold the largest private land auction in the area, selling off the lots to the highest bidders. Duson was sure his plan would work.

Duson, one of the largest landowners and rice growers in southwest Louisiana, was well-known throughout the area as a rough and tough adventurer who had enlisted in the home guards, Company D, Seventh Louisiana Cavalry, of the Confederacy at the beginning of the Civil War. During the war, his company was captured and held at New Orleans until the close of the war. By 1866, Duson was deputy sheriff of St. Landry Parish, under Sheriff Hayes, who had been captain of the home guards unit in which Duson had served during the Civil War. In 1873, Duson was elected sheriff of Landry Parish and served for fourteen years. He resigned this post when he was elected to the office of state senator. As sheriff, Duson was fearless and untiring in his pursuit of criminals, chasing outlaws from rural Louisiana to the borders of Mexico and to the mountains of the Indian Territory and even into Illinois. He was often the target of desperate shoot-outs as criminals fought capture and justice. Everyone had followed his law enforcement career as he tracked and ultimately brought down the Guilroy brothers, noted criminals who had long defied the law, in a shoot-out in Catahoula Parish. Tales of his pursuits of Louis Rousseau, guilty of murder in the Creek Nation, and John Slade, wanted for a heinous crime, were legendary. By 1888, the now-Louisiana senator persistently fought legislative battles and voluntarily retired four years later to pursue the development of the southwest area of the state he loved so much. His enterprises had included founding towns and bringing railroad lines to those small communities.

The plan at hand included advertising and promoting the upcoming land auction throughout the state. Duson enticed buyers to the area by offering free rides on the recently completed spur of the Southern Pacific Railroad. Special excursion trains ran through the countryside, transporting potential landowners north from the overcrowded city of New Orleans. People came from nearly every parish of the state, and a few even came from the neighboring states of Texas, Mississippi, and Alabama. Duson promised everyone who showed up a lavish barbecue banquet, live music, festive dancing, and close-up views of the "iron horse," an icon of progress that few had seen so up close.

The day was still and muggy and, like most other September days, hot. It had rained for nearly three straight days, making travel difficult, but by daybreak it was obvious that Duson's promotions were successful. Within hours, over four thousand people had gathered around the train depot. It was September 12, 1894, the day slated for the momentous land auction. Earlier in the day, C. C. Duson had submitted the paperwork necessary to charter the area as a village, naming it Eunice after his second and present wife, Eunice Pharr. He ceremoniously and dramatically drove a stake into the ground near the train depot and announced, "On this spot I will build a town."

Most people had come via the railroad, but more than fifteen hundred men and women had made the trek to Eunice, through mud and muck, on horseback, buggy, and wagon. Some had simply made the journey on foot. This once-in-a-lifetime opportunity to be a landowner was not to be missed just because of sloppy road conditions.

The village streets were suddenly alive with music. Ringing in the festivities was a brass band from nearby Crowley and a string band from the neighboring town of Rayne. Horses neighed, dogs barked, and children cried as noise levels increased. Even the flies seemed to be in a buzz of activity as visitors feasted on the promised tasty barbecue served from the roasting open pit. A *fais-do-do,* a lively community dance, was in full swing in the hall above Gus Fusilier's store, presently the only store in town. Men and women, hands together, whirled in time to the exuberant Cajun fiddlers stomping and grinding out favorite country tunes.

Then it was time. The officials mounted a flatbed car stationed on the railroad tracks. C. C. Duson welcomed locals and newcomers to the town of Eunice, announcing that they were here to have fun and purchase land for homes and businesses. Some public officials and state government bigwigs had been invited to the big event and they made exuberant and arousing speeches. Then Charles Garth, professional auctioneer, prepared to begin the auction in English while Gus Fusilier readied himself to hold the auction in French. Many of the people, especially those from areas surrounding Eunice, deep in Cajun country, could not speak a lick of English. Women in long prairie dresses and men in their Sunday best stood before the makeshift rostrum and waited for their turn to bid on a new homestead for their family. With each blow of the gavel, a completed sales transaction was marked and a new Eunice resident was applauded.

The auction was a huge success. The *Crowley Signal* ran the headline, "The Great Eunice Auction; a city is created!" Other papers reported that the property commanded fair prices and that day sales of $25,000 were recorded.

Within a year the village of Eunice had not only many new residents with modest homes but also two stores, a rice warehouse, and hotels. On June 4, 1895, Eunice was reincorporated as a newly chartered town. Just a week later, the first city council, overseen by Mayor Walter Duson, C. C. Duson's grown son, met to pass the first city ordinance.

Eunice, Louisiana's Prairie Cajun Capital, was on its way to becoming an influential city in the area in the two parishes it today straddles, Acadia and St. Landry. C. C. Duson went on to found the southwestern Louisiana towns of Iota in 1894 and Mamou in 1907.

In 1906 President Theodore Roosevelt appointed Duson a U.S. marshal for the Western District of Louisiana, a position he held until his death in New Orleans in 1910. The original train depot that was the backdrop for the 1894 homestead auction is today a museum of railroad artifacts, old toys, and Mardi Gras, pioneer farming, and Native American memorabilia. Cajun and zydeco music recordings are available in the museum's gift store.

FROGS RULED THE CITY

1901

Jacques Weil was quite intrigued when he received a letter from Rev. A. S. Doutre, a family friend who had just taken over as pastor of St. Joseph's Catholic Church in the small rural town of Rayne, Louisiana. Doutre's missive to his Parisian friends, the Weil brothers, who had immigrated to America in the late 1890s, described a virtual paradise. The brothers had been trying, without much success, to establish a business in Jackson, Mississippi. Doutre described the bounty of the area, the rich soil, and the abundance of game. He extolled the promise of a good future in Rayne, a French-speaking town about 150 miles west of New Orleans. But what really captured Weil's interest was the lucrative "frog"-exporting industry that he learned was exploding in the rural prairie town of Rayne. In his mind's eye, he could see a prosperous future for himself and his two brothers.

The early history of the area had led up to this propitious crossroad for the Weil brothers.

In 1852 the township of Queue Tortue, along the banks of the bayou of the same name, was established as a voting precinct in St.

Landry Parish. But in 1878 the town's post office was moved two miles north in the bayou settlement now referred to as Poupeville and closer to the church built three years earlier by Father Joseph Anthonioz, a Jesuit priest, on 162.25 acres purchased from the U.S. government. The area took its name from merchant Jules Poupeville, a French native who owned and operated a popular general store on public land that also served as a small stagecoach stop. The U.S. post office officially misspelled the name Pouppeville for the town with only 150 residents. But that was soon to change. In 1880, when the main line of the Louisiana Western Railroad bypassed Pouppeville, some houses and businesses were moved farther north to be near the railway. Dr. William H. Cunningham, employee of the railway and founder of the new town, named the station for railroad engineer B. W. L. Rayne.

Father Anthonioz was not willing to sacrifice his growing parish to remain in Pouppeville. He arranged for his church to be hoisted, placed on large wooden wheels, and hauled by teams of oxen to donated land in the new village, incorporated in 1883 as Rayne.

Just a few years later, Donat Pucheu arrived in town. Pucheu had been born in a small French village high in the Haute Pyrenees mountainous area of southwest France. When he came to America at the age of nineteen, he was looking for adventure. When he eventually found his way to Rayne in 1887, he was thirty-seven years old, married, and looking for a place to settle down. Pucheu was a fun-loving, jovial sort who loved life. Some say he was a gourmet chef; others, that he just enjoyed eating the best foods and drinking the finest wines. He and his wife, Marie Agnelly, loved to entertain guests for dinner, but he lamented that he could not offer his guests the "finest" epicurean delights in his Rayne homestead. Pucheu found a way to fix this.

He began taking the wild game he trapped in the dense swampy areas over to the world-famous New Orleans restaurants, trading them for imported cheeses, French wines, and hard-to-come-by Old World spices. One of the most sought-after critters by the haute cuisine French restaurants were the fat juicy bullfrogs that were so abundant in the swamps and bayou of southwestern Louisiana. Pucheu's success allowed him to expand his trading business. The transcontinental Southern Pacific Railroad had purchased the Louisiana Western in 1881, connecting Rayne to not only to nearby New Orleans markets but also to both coasts and the many cities and towns in between.

The stage was set for Jacques Weil's entrance into Rayne. Jacques took Reverend Doutre's advice and moved to Rayne in 1901 eager to make his fortune. He founded and became senior partner in the general store of Jacques Weil, Boudreaux and Leger. His brother Edmond also came to Rayne with his wife and son. Brother Gontran came, too, alone and would never marry. Jacques sent for and soon married the love of his life, Mathilde Langneau. Although his company mainly sold poultry, eggs, and produce to the New Orleans market, they were expanding to pecans, furs, wool, and turtles. But Jacques was intent on growing the frog-shipping business. He had some great ideas and was anxious to put them into practice.

Everyone knew there were frogs everywhere in the area. You could hear their eerie cacophony throughout the quiet, rural nights. Frogs loved the bug-infested marshes and thrived in the surrounding bayous, rice fields, swamps, and ponds. But what Jacques soon found out was that Rayne frogs were bigger than most species, and that meant they had more meat on their large legs, a surefire selling point.

Frog season began in late February and was at its peak in April. Jacques needed frog hunters. He found plenty of them. Trappers traipsed through the sluggish wetlands in the dark of night, shining their lighted lanterns toward the water. Frogs froze when they saw bright light, making them easy to capture and plop into waiting burlap sacks. All across Acadia Parish, humid spring nights belonged to the lantern-toting hunters searching the darkness for the elusive *Rana catesbeiana*. The next morning, full sacks of frogs were deposited at the store, in exchange for groceries or small change to gamble away playing *boureé*.

Behind the store, Weil installed a large chicken-wire pen to be used as a "frog aquarium." This frog storage coop could hold up to fifteen thousand *ouaouarons*, the local word for the bullfrogs whose onomatopoeic pronunciation is explained by the Cajun dictionary as "wawaron." When the cage was full, as it most often was, a five-man cleaning crew was kept busy. Weil had bright lights erected above the cage, which attracted enough insects at night to feed the confined amphibians, keeping them alive before they faced the skinning knife in the morning. Some say if skinners found any suffocated frogs in the cages in the morning, Weil directed them to "kill the dead ones first."

Live frogs were shipped to nearby New Orleans markets, but those bound for further cities such as Houston were first killed and cleaned in Rayne and then the legs were put on ice for shipping. But the legs were not the only parts of the frogs that brought a fair price. The hides were valuable as well. When frogs were butchered on company premises, the hides were slung into large barrels, and then they were covered with salt and sent to tanneries to become purses, wallets, and other leather goods. Barrels of hides could weigh up to three hundred pounds.

Jacques' business empire grew. The newly formed J. & E. Weil Operating Company owned cotton gins, a rice mill, and a theater. Jacques looked around one day and smiled at his success. He was full owner of the Jacques Weil Frog Shipping Company and the Weil General Merchandise Store. His company was shipping ten thousand pounds of frog legs from Rayne a week. The local papers reported the number and weights of frog shipments through the train depot in Rayne as regular items of business. The Louisiana town was famous worldwide for supplying barrels and barrels of frog legs to gourmet restaurants across the United States, from St. Louis to Los Angeles, and even to the European continent. "Rayne frog legs" were on the menus of the most exclusive restaurants in France. They were also served at Sardi's in New York City.

But good things don't always last. When war-driven high agricultural prices dropped at the end of World War I, many farm-products brokers were ruined. The Hibernia Bank of New Orleans purchased the bankrupt Weil brothers' assets, including the frog business. But Jacques was not done yet. He jumped right back into the frog business, going up against stiff competitors who were fighting for a share of the frog-shipping business.

Eventually the frog business passed on from its glory days. The local rice fields and bayous around Rayne could no longer supply the demand. Weil tried his hand at trucking in frogs captured in the Atchafalaya Basin, the swamps near New Orleans, and the Sabine River estuaries, and even from as far away as Mississippi and Arkansas, but the frog industry was doomed. Cheaper frogs from overseas and local habitat degradation meant little profit for the frog hunters and merchants. The once-massive trade to restaurants around the world became a small-time business supplying biology lab specimens and subjects for NASA space experiments.

Jacques Weil passed away in 1948. But his frog-leg legacy remains. Rayne is today called the "Frog Capital of the World," and frog murals adorn stores and businesses throughout the city. Its annual Frog Festival and Frog Derby are much-touted Labor Day weekend events, but if you go, be sure not to park illegally, or, as the signs say, you might get "toad away."

HEYWOOD'S HEYDAY

1901

Southern Louisiana Indian folklore mentions using oil found in natural seeps for medicinal purposes. In 1540, Hernando DeSoto and his explorers called the rich, tar-like substance seeping out of the marshy areas along the Mississippi River "stone pitch" and used it to caulk their boats for water tightness.

More than 350 years later, on a warm, not especially significant day in 1901, Jules Clément looked out over his property situated on a noticeable rise in an otherwise flat area called the "Mamou Prairie." His family had owned this land near the village of Evangeline for nearly a hundred years. He noticed some small bubbles rising from a recently flooded rice field. Stories of Spindletop, the successful well drilled atop a Beaumont salt dome less than a year earlier, piqued his interest. The high ground was similar to Spindletop, where the erupting Lucas Gusher had sent mud, rock, oil, and even drill pipe into the air.

Clément rushed to his farm, grabbed an old stovepipe, and hurried back to the rice field. He knew natural gas was almost always an indicator of oil reserves. He stood the stovepipe in the ground where he had seen the bubbles, lit a match, and threw it down into the pipe. The gas ignited.

Clément began to talk in town of his discovery. As word spread, Stanley A. Spencer, Frank R. Jaenke, Thomas C. Mahaffey, Avery C. Wilkins, and I. D. L. Williams, a group of businessmen from Jennings, quickly organized the S. A. Spencer Co. Thinking they might have a repeat of Spindletop in their own backyard, the group quietly negotiated leases to land in the vicinity, including Clément's forty acres. After the leases were signed, the company hired the Heywood Company, successful drillers of Spindletop, to look at the property and assess if finding oil was a possibility.

Clément had a change of heart. He suddenly didn't want any wells drilled on land that had been in his family since the early 1800s. He padlocked the gates to his fenced property, making the excuse that if wells were drilled on his property, his cows would fall into the holes and break their legs. He added, parenthetically, that he wouldn't know what to do with oil, should any be discovered on his land.

Heywood arrived on the scene and noted the land formation was very much like the salt dome of Spindletop. However, he realized that his first order of business would be to convince Clément. Heywood had been savvy enough to bring an interpreter with him, for Clément spoke only French. Clément listened carefully to Heywood's assurances that the cattle would not be harmed in any way. To circumvent Clément's argument that he didn't know what to do with his share of the oil, Heywood promised to act as a selling agent for the oil at no cost to Clément. Then Clément argued that the government would take most of his money in taxes, so drilling probably wasn't worth the effort. Heywood told Clément that the lease would be written so that the Heywood Company would pay all taxes. Clément was on a roll.

When Heywood promised to pay Clément generously for any damage to his cattle, rice fields, or crops, Clément relented. A self-satisfied smile showed he was a tough, and pretty smart, negotiator.

Heywood conducted his own tests on the property by putting a match to the bubbles. When he saw a red flame, with smoke at the top, he knew it was petroleum gas. A contract calling for two wells, each to be drilled to one thousand feet, was signed. If the first well did not produce oil at one thousand feet, the well would be closed and a second well would be started.

All the necessary rig equipment, drilling machinery, and pipe were hauled from Beaumont's Spindletop to the site of the Heywood #1 Jules Clément well. On June 5, 1901, the derrick reached sixty-four feet in the air and drilling commenced. Jennings, population 1,539 in the 1900 census, served as the home-office base for the state's first oilfield workers.

Drilling in south Louisiana was a curiosity, and people waited anxiously for news of the impending gusher. As the depth of the well reached eight hundred feet, then nine hundred feet, nerves were frayed. When oil was not discovered at one thousand feet, most speculated the well was a bust. Though the well was contractually set to be abandoned, Heywood had a gut feeling the oil was there. He instructed the crew to keep drilling.

It had been nearly three months since the drilling had begun, and as the fifteen-hundred-foot mark loomed with little evidence of a gusher, many investors pulled their support, selling their $1 shares for as little as $.25. Time meant money, and the Jennings well was becoming very expensive. Heywood's associates and the drilling crew urged him to abandon the venture. But he wouldn't.

As the well passed the fifteen-hundred-foot mark, any hope left was dying. When the crew ran out of drill pipe, it was decision-making time! Abandon the well or get more supplies? Heywood wanted to continue and ordered more drill pipe for the Jennings Field. The percussion-drilling drill bit was hoisted up over and over again, then dropped in a free fall into the well. The force of impact from the massive drill bit broke rock lying at the bottom of the hole. The pounding halted every so often so a scooping bailer could be lowered into the hole to remove the rock debris.

The slow, tedious process continued. Sixteen hundred feet! Still no sign of any gushing oil. Nearing seventeen hundred feet, with only four feet to go on the last piece of available drilling pipe, Heywood felt the "sugar sand" soil was showing good signs of oil. Again he ordered additional drill pipe. The seventeen-hundred-foot mark was reached and passed. At eighteen hundred feet, there was still no oil, but the pounding continued. Finally, at 1,832 feet—eureka! After bailing the well, a four-inch gusher of oil flowed a hundred feet in the air, drenching Clément's rice fields with a layer of oil for over seven hours. Several acres of Clément's rice fields were ruined, but he wasn't worried, because he knew he would be reimbursed for the damage by Heywood.

On September 21, 1901, a local farmer rushed into Jennings with the news that oil had been discovered.

"Oil Fever" had begun! Scores of wells sprang up almost overnight. By the summer of 1902, Jennings oil was being loaded onto Southern Pacific tank cars for distribution to the rest of the country. Oil was also transported by barges and tugs owned and operated by the Heywood Transportation Co. via the nearby Mermentau River. The wells were producing more oil than the pipeline could handle. The Heywood brothers hired a Houston contractor to dig a series of holding pits in the ground to store millions of barrels of oil. The well continued to produce about seven thousand barrels of oil a day. The Jennings Field has produced more than 120 million barrels of oil and 45 billion cubic feet of gas since 1901. Until the 1920s, this accounted for 67 percent of Louisiana's total oil and gas usage.

Jennings is called the "Cradle of Louisiana Oil," and a replica of the oil rig used to drill the first productive oil well in the state can be seen in the Oil and Gas Park in Jennings. The first refinery was built in Baton Rouge in 1909; today, it is the largest oil refinery on the North American continent. The offshore-drilling industry was born in 1934 when the Texas Company drilled a well in the Gulf of Mexico, one mile off the Louisiana shoreline.

JUNGLE MAN COMES TO TOWN

1917

The buzz around town was that Hollywood bigwigs were coming to small-town, rural Morgan City, Louisiana, to make a movie. It was 1917 and the film industry was still in its infancy—silent movies ruled. Word was there would be paying jobs for locals in the "jungle" scenes, including roles as "extras" for black residents. Jobs were sorely needed as people eked out meager livings in the small, backwoods town hugging the banks of the Atchafalaya River. The Attakapas Indians had named the 135-mile waterway and the largest swamp basin in the United States the Atchafalaya, meaning "long river."

Morgan City was originally named Tigre Island because of the "tiger-resembling" type of wildcats reportedly seen in the area by land surveyors in the early 1800s. By 1860, the town had changed its name and incorporated as Brashear City, named after Walter Brashear, a prominent Kentuckian who had bought large tracts of land for his sugar mills. During the Civil War, Union soldiers at Fort Starr planned and carried out the destruction of the salt mines on Avery Island and put an end to Confederate resistance in the area.

In 1876 the town took its present name, Morgan City, a tribute to railroad and steamship tycoon Charles Morgan, who had dredged the Atchafalaya Bay Ship Channel to allow oceangoing vessels to reach the port city.

But all the name changes did little to bring sustained prosperity to the river community. Having a film production crew come to town was a big deal. But what sort of movie wanted the dense, moss-laden landscape as a backdrop and black folks as actors?

A few years earlier, door-to-door salesman Edgar Rice Burroughs had had enough of selling pencil sharpeners. The former Army private, cowboy, prospector, shop clerk, and accountant turned his hand to writing. His first published story in 1912 was about an aristocratic couple, Lord and Lady Greystroke, who had been put ashore in West Africa after a ship mutiny in 1886. They built a hut, managed to survive for a while, and had a son. After his mother died of a fever and his father was killed by Mangani apes, the youngster was taken in and raised by the same Mangani tribe, an advanced group of apes with limited language abilities. Called Tarzan, the boy grew to manhood among the apes and eventually found a love interest, Jane, who appeared on the African scene with her father, a debt-ridden adventurer following a treasure map of the Dark Continent. The wild adventure tale, published in *All-Story Magazine* in October 1912, was an immediate success and two years later was published in book form. Burroughs dashed off twenty-six more books about Tarzan's adventures. The Tarzan story caught the attention of the film industry, and plans to shoot the movie were put in motion.

Everyone was excited about the film being made in Morgan City, chosen because of the surrounding jungle-like swamps, the large number of African Americans who could be enticed to work as extras, and the nearby rail line, which could transport film crews, sets, and equipment from California.

Many of the scenes of *Tarzan of the Apes* were shot deep in the Atchafalaya River basin. The mainly Cajun population in the area wasn't too sure the Hollywood people were ready for the harsh conditions of the swamp areas. Louisiana's subtropical climate could be treacherous. Some cases of malaria were reported among the crew members, and infestations of red bugs were not uncommon. But most agreed Morgan City offered African jungle-like areas without filmmakers actually having to cross the ocean. The dense river basin was replete with wildlife, wild scrub vegetation, towering cypress trees, and thick trailing vines.

Tarzan portrayer Elmo Lincoln, born Otto Elmo Likenhelt, had been tapped for the role by D. W. Griffith, who noted the apt muscularity of the Californian stevedore. Lincoln loved the Louisiana landscape and was challenged to fulfill Burroughs' depiction of his character: "He could spring twenty feet across space at the dizzy heights of the forest top and grasp with unerring precision, and without apparent jar, a limb waving wildly in the path of an approaching tornado." Lincoln liked the pristine jungle landscape of bent and fallen trees that allowed him to run along large tree trunks instead of climbing up them.

During late summer of 1917, the Tarzan film crew entrenched in Morgan City daily boarded a small steamboat and headed down Bayou Teche six or so miles to the Atchafalaya River swamp. The bayou's name, "Teche," is thought to come from the Chitimacha Indian word "tenche," meaning "snake," reflecting the bayou's twists and turns through which waters flow, resembling a snake's movement. Other scenes were shot south of Morgan City on Avoca Island, home to the sugarcane plantations where most of the eight hundred African Americans who played the natives in the film lived and worked. The only access to this island was by a floating pier ferry with a small engine that was pulled on steel cables to get from one bank to the other. On the island, crew and actors were trucked overland to film sets. A native village was erected in Morgan City's Lake End Park to be burned in the climax of the film.

Local industries were also excited about cashing in on the movie being filmed in the area. The Shannon Hardware store at the corner of Front and Everett was rented out to the film's producers for a studio. In another part of the building, tailors and seamstresses were busy making ape costumes to be worn by the six or eight professional circus acrobats and about thirty New Orleans Athletic Club gymnasts brought to Morgan City to play jungle creatures. Complaints about the ape costumes, which were made of goat hide and a sponge material, were rampant. It seems they were so hot the actors could stand to be in them for only a minute or two. More than twenty live apes and monkeys were also brought in for realism and to give the scene an authentic African look. Rumor had it that a lion, said to have turned violent on set, was killed by Lincoln, but the rumor that really set tongues wagging in Morgan City was the claim by old locals that some of the monkeys brought in for the film were left behind and still roam the Atchafalaya swamp today.

Boat owners and operators at the time jumped at the opportunity to earn additional income. A specially designed moss-harvesting boat was used to help out with the logistics of moving men and materials along the waterways. This homemade craft, built in the late 1800s out of one piece of cypress, was capable of gathering five hundred pounds of swamp moss from the trees for pillow and mattress stuffing. This boat was used decades later in the filming of *The Curious Case of Benjamin Button*. Other sites in Morgan City, the Jungle Gardens and the Costello Hotel, where the actors and actresses stayed, unfortunately no longer exist.

Tarzan of the Apes, the first Tarzan film ever produced, was released on January 27, 1918, in New York City, as a silent film with

English intertitles. It was directed by Scott Sidney and starred Elmo Lincoln as Tarzan and Enid Markey as Jane. The movie is based on the first part of Burroughs' book *Tarzan of the Apes*, and the second part of his novel would appear in film as *The Romance of Tarzan*. Tarzan remains an international phenomenon. *Tarzan of the Apes* was one of the first films to make over $1 million in profit and the first feature film shot on location in the United States. More than forty feature films connected to Tarzan's story have been made and nearly 250 live and animated television shows have been produced. Future projects are in the wings, including a new feature film and a comic strip series.

Father-and-daughter documentary team Al and Allison Bohl spent years researching the first Tarzan film shot in Morgan City. Their documentary, *Tarzan: Lord of the Louisiana Jungle*, previewed at the 2012 Tarzan festival, which celebrated the hundredth anniversary of Burroughs' first Tarzan story. The festival included the opening of the Tarzan exhibit at the Patterson State Museum, which features vintage Tarzan memorabilia. Burroughs was an early pioneer in releasing film-related promotional items. His licensing company brought Tarzan bread, Tarzan gasoline, and Tarzan glue to the American people. Festivalgoers can take Cajun Jack's Swamp Tour (www.cajunjack.com) of scenes from the film, participate in a Tarzan yelling contest, or enter a Tarzan and Jane look-alike contest. Governor Bobby Jindal proclaimed April 13, 2012, as Tarzan Day in Louisiana.

BOLL WEEVILS BUILD AN AIRLINE

1922

The cotton was high and nearing picking time, but, once again, the crop was threatened by the hungry boll weevil, insidious little pests of 1/8" to 1/3" in length plaguing farmers throughout the state of Louisiana. Something had to be done to stop the native insect of Central America, which had crossed the Rio Grande into the United States back in the early 1890s. Increasing in numbers every year, the boll weevil, *Anthonomus grandis Boheman*, invaded fields, fed on cotton buds and flowers, and devastated cotton crops across the South. By 1908, the cotton crop in Madison Parish was only 60 percent of the previous year. Cotton farmers were in crisis mode, and often entire fields had to be abandoned due to the infestations.

The situation was so severe that the government stepped in to find some relief for the farmers. In 1909, R. A. Cushman was sent to look for a place to build a research lab to address the farmers' concerns with the boll weevil. He carefully surveyed much of northern Louisiana and decided that Madison Parish would be the ideal place for a research facility. Tallulah, the parish seat of Madison Parish, bordered the Mississippi River and had a good amount of rainfall, moderate temperatures, and areas of dense timber draped with Spanish moss, where boll weevils naturally hibernated. This area was typical of the hundreds of thousands of acres of infested cotton fields throughout the Deep South, and so it was here he established the Tallulah Laboratory, Southern Field Crop Insect Investigations, Bureau of Entomology, U.S. Department of Agriculture.

Finding a way to destroy the devastating beetles was not to be achieved quickly, and there was still much work to be done when G. D. Smith replaced Cushman in 1910; he was succeeded by Bert R. Coad in 1915.

The Tallulah research lab, referred to as the Delta Laboratory, set up a model village for boll weevil residents. Cages of small structures adorned with Spanish moss, cotton stalks, bare dirt, and sawmill shavings held five hundred boll weevils each. Here the critters were propagated and raised to adulthood. Their appetites, habits, and the effects of various insecticides were studied, and changes in their life and development were recorded.

The work was extremely slow. Coad was assisted by entomologist Collett E. Woolman, district supervisor for the Louisiana State University agricultural extension service. Convinced that the answer to the boll weevil problem would be found in toxic chemicals, they brought in chemists and engineers who designed and developed various types of poison-dispensing machines. Many of the experiments to control the boll weevil used lead arsenate, a poison already in use in other areas of the country to control various pests, with unsatisfactory results.

The lab was staffed with over one hundred people working to find a better solution, and in the end the researchers and scientists prevailed. Eureka! It was at the Delta Laboratory that calcium arsenate was first found to be more effective against Public Enemy No. 1 of the cotton crop than any other poison!

At first, calcium arsenate was a crude product, but work continued to stabilize the chemical compound. In 1916 and 1917, small test plots were successfully treated with calcium arsenate. The next year, thirty-five thousand acres of cotton crops were dusted under the supervision of the Bureau of Entomology. The satisfactory results led manufacturers to produce about three million pounds of calcium arsenate in 1919, ten million pounds in 1920, and sixty to seventy million pounds a year in ensuing seasons until synthetic organic insecticides became available in the late 1940s.

But the farmers' problems were not over yet. Applying the deadly powdery insecticide was problematic. At first the calcium arsenate was spread through the fields by mules with a hickory pole with gunny sacks full of poison on the ends attached to the animals' backs. The mules were trotted down the rows of cotton, jolting the insecticide out of the sacks. Abandoning this primitive process, laborers began to sprinkle the compound with a blower or rotary "handgun" as they traipsed through the fields or sat atop a mule-drawn wagon or tractor, but the handgun had a small dispersion range and proved to be very time consuming. To spray several rows of cotton plants at a time, farmers tried bundling several insecticide gun nozzles together and mounting them on a dray that could be pulled by one or two mules. But this unwieldy apparatus was too labor intensive. A motorized machine was experimented with, but the complex skills needed to run it were not in the purview of most farmers. Gasoline-powered engines were developed to operate fans that would distribute the poison, but this was still an impractical application method for most planters.

Necessity is the mother of invention, and new technology was waiting in the wings for just such a necessity as controlling the boll weevil. In 1922, airplanes had successfully been used in a government program in Ohio to dust catalpa trees for sphinx moths. When news of this breakthrough reached Dr. Coad at the Delta Lab in Tallulah, he rushed to Washington, D.C., and requested government funding, along with planes, pilots, and mechanics of the Army Air Service, to experiment with crop-dusting calcium arsenate in Louisiana. Six men and three planes (two Curtiss Jennys with one Dehaviland 4-B) arrived at the one-hundred-acre tract of land on Shirley Plantation near Tallulah that had been readied as an airstrip. The land was owned by the estate of W. M. Scott, and the airport, the first municipal airport in Louisiana, was named Scott Field in his honor. Scott Field had a hangar, storage space for fuel and chemicals, a weather observatory, and a Standard Zenith Airway Beacon light that made six turns per minute and was visible for forty-five miles.

Coad was very interested in aeronautics, and Woolman, an avid aviator, had attended the world's first aviation meet in Rheims, France, in 1909. Together the two men embarked on early aerial experiments with crop dusting that involved dumping calcium arsenate out of sacks from the sides of the planes. Their next improvement was to move the gas tanks of the plane over a bit and install a hopper from which to release the pesticide. When early pilots in single-engine Jennys made their runs over the infested cotton fields, they would pull a lever releasing the calcium carbonate. Unfortunately, the compound would often billow back up into the pilot's face, nearly choking him.

But fate soon played its hand in developing modern aviation when by coincidence George B. Post, vice president of Huff Daland and Company, a New York airplane manufacturer, made an unscheduled stop at Scott Field to deal with his plane's mechanical problems. He heard about the work being done at the Tallulah lab and was intrigued. He spent many hours observing Coad and Woolman's work at the lab, envisioning crop dusting as a new market for selling his airplanes. Almost immediately, the Huff Daland Company started building the Huff Daland Duster, the first plane specifically designed for crop dusting. Various models were tested at Scott Field, replacing the antiquated postwar government planes. The first crop duster to combat the boll weevil was named "The Puffer" due to the plane's quite visible emanation of white clouds of pesticide. The planes bore a logo depicting Thor, the Norse god of thunder, blowing on cotton fields. The world's first commercial aerial crop-dusting company was born, and, more importantly, the boll weevil would never be allowed to ruin one of the most important cash crops of the South ever again.

In 1925, to market aerial dusting directly to farmers, the Huff Daland Company hired Woolman to head up a separate crop-dusting division in Monroe. Woolman left science and joined the company as operations manager and salesman. The company used freelance aviators, barnstormers, and military pilots on leave. These airmen, in leather jackets and goggles, excitedly grinning from open cockpits, gave rise to the adventure-seeking image of early airmen. Reputations as risky daredevils, skirting treetops and filling the sky with barrel rolls, front and back loops, and dives, were earned, and their expertise at skimming the white pods of the cotton plants with the wheels of their crop dusters was legendary.

Advertisements in local newspapers invited farmers to free demonstrations of "Dusting by Aeroplane." "The Puffer" also ferried single passengers around the southeastern states. For this dual purpose a passenger chair was anchored in the bin where the insecticide was usually kept.

In 1928, something else "happened" that made national history. Times were tough financially for the Huff Daland Company, and it was ready to close its Louisiana crop-dusting division of Dusters. Woolman came to the rescue. He raised $40,000 from local investors to buy the company and start his own business. But it needed a name. He wanted something that would reflect the Mississippi River's influence on the Arkansas–Mississippi–Louisiana region. Company executive secretary Catherine Fitzgerald suggested "Delta," and Delta

Air Service was born. Delta ordered three Curtiss-Wright Travel Air S-6000B monoplanes. Touted as the "Limousine of the Air," the Travel Air could cruise at ninety miles per hour with a flying range of five hundred miles. Delta's new triangle logo replaced the old puffing Norse god, and the motto "Speed, Safety and Comfort" was adopted.

On June 17, 1929, Delta's first passenger service departed from Dallas' Love Field with five passengers aboard. Johnny Howe, a trim stunt pilot from Arkansas with slicked-down hair and popular pencil-thin moustache, taxied down the runaway at 8:00 a.m. The plane stopped in Shreveport and in Monroe, Louisiana, at Delta's headquarters, and landed in Jackson, Mississippi, to a crowd-filled airstrip replete with festive banners and congratulatory signs. Newspapers touted the Travel Air's inner "soundproof" cabin that made conversation during flight possible and noted that roll-down windows allowed passengers an option for ventilation. The Dallas–Jackson round-trip fare was $90.

At the airport in Monroe, passengers stepped up to the plane right next to Delta's one-story stucco headquarters. A sign read, "DANGER—Beware of Propeller," but passengers often helped spin the propeller to start the motor. No flight attendants offered food or beverage service, but stationmasters at the airports always had free coffee available. Catherine "Miss Fitz" Fitzgerald and a collie named Brownie were Delta's official greeters in Monroe. Surprisingly, the planes had no two-way radios. Weather reports and landing access were radio-telegraphed back and forth between the airports and planes.

The era that saw the success of the Delta Air Duster Division ended in 1966; the company's closing coincided with the deaths of Coad and Woolman. Five years later, on June 30, 1973, after sixty-four years of continuous operation, the USDA Cotton Insects Research Laboratory in Tallulah, Louisiana, closed as well. "The

Puffer," the first plane specifically designed for crop-dusting the boll weevil, is now in the Southern Museum of Flight. The cotton insect research laboratory's building built by the Standard Oil Company at Scott's Field is today listed on the National Register of Historic Buildings.

CANADIAN HUSKY FINDS ETERNAL
REST IN LOUISIANA SOIL

1931

The children were excited to see Unalaska, one of Admiral Richard E. Byrd's lead sled dogs. They had studied his 1928–1930 expeditions to the South Pole in history class and knew the explorations had been made by snowshoe, snowmobile, airplane . . . and dogsled.

Monroe residents couldn't believe that their small town was on the itinerary for the triumphant cross-country tour to celebrate the expedition's accomplishments. Admiral Byrd would give public lectures, and the locals could meet the famous sled dogs. Unalaska, former lead dog and star attraction, was part of the canine corps.

As adults made plans to attend Byrd's talks, local children eagerly awaited the appearance of the pure-white husky always at the great admiral's side. This type of dog had not heretofore been seen in the hot, humid region of the Deep South. The curious folks didn't know that five-year-old Unalaska was not a purebred husky, but rather a mix of wolf, St. Bernard, Setter, and Siberian husky. But, they did know that Unalaska had lived an adventurous life and was hailed as a hero. Unalaska, born in 1923 in the Northwest Territories of Canada near the Mackenzie River, the largest river flowing into the Arctic from North America, had been personally handpicked by Byrd. Unalaska was proud to be the lead dog and worked hard in the Antarctic region to make his master proud.

By the end of December 1930, Admiral Byrd and his entourage were in Monroe, in Ouachita Parish of northeast Louisiana. The residents were excited that such a famous explorer was in their midst. Schoolchildren looked forward to meeting the dogs and hearing the stories of the great expedition. It was the dogs, of course, that stole their hearts, especially the personable and energetic Unalaska. But being confined and constantly leashed made the dogs rambunctious and antsy. On January 3, Carroll B. Foster, manager of the exhibit and tour, took Unalaska and Lady for some exercise in Forsythe Park. Lady and Unalaska were canine friends and loved playing together; if you saw one, you found the other. However, this Saturday afternoon would never be forgotten by the many townspeople who had gathered to watch the dogs romp in the park. Lady headed across Riverside Drive with Unalaska following closely behind. Foster called out to the dogs, beckoning them to come back to the park. Lady made it safely back across the street, but tragedy struck her loyal friend. A Chevrolet Coupe heading down the road hit and killed Unalaska, hauling his body over fifty feet. As the crowd of children and adults watched, the driver panicked, pulled his hat down low over his eyes to hide his face, and kept driving. Unalaska's hit-and-run killer was never caught.

Unalaska's death made national news. Admiral Byrd was brokenhearted. Not too long ago he had buried another favorite sled dog, Igloo, who had gotten sick and died. He still remembered the small white casket with silver handles as it was lowered into the ground in a pet cemetery in Boston. Byrd's epitaph to his dear friend,

"Igloo—More than a Friend," was engraved on the dog's marble grave marker.

The devastated community wanted to do something big to mark the famous dog's passing in their town. When Admiral Byrd agreed to let Unalaska rest in peace in Monroe, plans were put in place for a virtual state funeral for the beloved dog. Julia Wossman, renowned educator and elementary school principal, stepped up and took charge to arrange the grand funeral ceremony. A small white velvet-lined casket adorned with pink satin cushions was chosen to hold Unalaska's remains, which would be embalmed by the Cory-Davis Funeral Parlor in town.

The city granted permission for Unalaska to be buried on the lawn of the American Legion B. L. Faulk Post 13 at 401 Forsythe Avenue near the ill-fated Forsythe Park. An afternoon of events was planned. The city' schools closed at 2:00 p.m. so Monroe schoolchildren could participate in the ceremonies. Over three thousand children took part in the procession and, along with mourning Monroe citizens, filed past Unalaska's coffin, where local Boy Scouts formed an honor guard. At the ceremony, two polar expedition dogs stood at attention with Admiral Byrd and other dignitaries as children stood on tiptoes, craning their necks to see what was going on. Carroll Foster gave the eulogy as Unalaska's casket, covered with flowers, was lowered into the ground between two French artillery guns that had seen service during World War I. A tree was planted in memory of Unalaska at the foot of his grave. The flag flying over the American Legion post was ceremoniously lowered to half-mast out of respect for the cherished lead dog.

Though there was some controversy over the canine being buried on the hallowed ground of World War I veterans, there were still more memorials to be awarded Unalaska. On July 9, 1931, six months after Unalaska's burial, Young Armand McHenry Jr. gave a memorial address and two little girls, Martha Chambers and Marilyn Bush, standing one on either side of the stone memorial, raised a white veil to reveal a memorial stone marker. The seven-hundred-pound Indiana limestone monument was donated by the company building the new Ernest Long Neville High School, a modernistic structure designed by Merl Padgett, just two blocks down Forsythe Avenue from the American Legion hall. A bronze plaque inscribed with Unalaska's name and history was donated by the J. M. Supply Company. The plaque read: "Sacred to the memory of Unalaska, killed by automobile in this city Jan. 3, 1931, a dog of the Byrd Antarctic expedition, whose dauntless courage played an important part in that great scientific adventure. 'A great leader and a true friend—he never turned back,'—Admiral Byrd. Erected by the school children of the city of Monroe."

But Unalaska was not to rest in peace. The next morning, amid increased tension and bitter arguments among those who were proud that Unalaska had been laid to rest on the grounds of the American Legion and others who thought the dog's burial was disrespectful to fallen heroes, the monument was stolen. Residents were stunned to discover the marker was gone. The heavy stone marker had been crushed, destroyed, and hauled away. Only small fragments of the stone were left behind. Rumors circulated that the memorial pieces had been thrown in the Ouachita River a few blocks to the west. In any case, the marker was never recovered.

Julia Wossman again took charge and led a student committee at the Georgia Tucker School, a beautifully designed building in the Italian Renaissance and Romanesque style, to raise money for a new marker. Fearing further destruction and sensing the ominous mood of the veterans' groups, Unalaska's casket was dug up and, with approval from city officials, moved to the grounds of the red-tiled Tucker school on Stubbs Avenue just blocks from Forsythe Park.

Unalaska was buried in a second funeral ceremony. The new marble monument was engraved with a likeness of the beloved husky and an inscription that reads: "Unalaska, a husky of Admiral Richard E. Byrd, South Pole Expedition, buried here. Jan. 1931."

The Alaskan Husky was adopted as the school's team mascot. (Go, Alaskan Huskies!) Unalaska is still guarding the entrance of the school far from his mushing detail in the frozen land that brought him historical recognition. Though the school was closed in 1999, its corner towers with triple-arch windows and Persian columns are still noteworthy. And if you walk up to the old school on the Stubbs Avenue side, you can see the celebrated headstone of Unalaska, placed lovingly among the flower beds by tearful schoolchildren over eighty years ago.

PLAYING FOR THE CHAMPIONSHIP

1932

The Fourth of July weekend was at hand. For the black population of Monroe, Louisiana, a staunchly segregated town of twenty-six thousand residents in the rural northeastern part of the state, there were no scheduled civic activities planned for the nation's birthday celebration. The children's bicycle parade, the bathing suit fashion show, and the swim races at the town pool were strictly for the white folks. But those events and the underlying racial tensions of a divided town, known for vigilante lynching and poor race relations, didn't matter much when baseball was in town. Differences were swept under the heavy hometown dirt when the Monarchs, a national-caliber Negro League baseball team, was set to play.

Baseball had become a popular sport, thanks in part to new hitter-friendly rules, which led to the rise of famous "sluggers" like Babe Ruth, and to the new medium of radio, which broadcast games across the airwaves. As in many other small towns across America, the hot summer days brought out Monroe's avid baseball fans—of all races.

Despite the ongoing Depression, Monroe had experienced a recent boon to its economy. A 425-square-mile gas field, one of the largest in the country, had been discovered. By 1932, 876 gas wells had been completed in the area, yielding already 1,592 billion cubic feet of gas. The prospect of tapping and bringing to market all things connected to the gas industry had brought both whites and blacks to the area looking for fame and fortune. Hundreds of jobs were available and most of those were offered by millionaire natural gas and oil man, Fred Stovall, a Texan who had moved to Monroe to start the Stovall Drilling Company. Stovall made gobs of money in the gas and oil business and was respected and befriended by most people in the industry, including his day laborers. He started several new oil- and gas-related businesses that were very successful.

But baseball was his true love. To keep up the morale of his J. M. Supply Company's large contingency of workers and to feed his passion for baseball, Stovall formed and financed an all-black baseball team. The minor league team was entirely made up of Stovall's most athletic black employees. To provide a place to play and practice, Stovall built Casino Park, a baseball field near his plantation just outside Monroe city limits in the Booker T. Washington district. He also built other recreational facilities, including a swimming pool and dance pavilion. These amenities, used only by the black population of Monroe, were considered very fine and were much appreciated by the locals. The players lived in houses on Stovall's plantation and meals were prepared by a hired cook. In 1932 Stovall bought the team three new Fords for traveling. But, most importantly reported the team, he always paid his players.

On May 11, 1930, the Monarchs played its inaugural game as a Texas–Louisiana League team. The team's first manager, Alonzo Longware Jr., put pitcher Barney Morris on the mound in an away game against New Jersey's Newtown Braves, and the Monarchs won

5–4. The first game played in Casino Park was against the Lake Charles Giants before fifteen hundred fans. The Monarchs won 4–3. After the Monarchs won the 1931 Texas–Louisiana series championship, Stovall began to formulate bigger plans for his team. He wanted the Monarchs to move up to the major leagues. When the Negro National League did not field a schedule for the 1932 season, Stovall's Monarchs and four other teams formed the Negro Southern League, which became a "major" league of Negro League baseball along with the East-West Colored League (which collapsed in early July 1932).

One of Stovall's first moves was to hire a business manager. He enticed H. D. "Doug" English from the Shreveport Sports, another Texas–Louisiana team, to join the Monarchs. The 1932 spring training began on March 5, and on March 24 a two-game exhibition match between the Monroe Monarchs and the Pittsburgh Crawfords, training in nearby Hot Springs, Arkansas, was played.

The Negro Southern League began its first regular season on Easter weekend. Though the Monarchs were considered the season's dark horse, they first beat the Greys at Little Rock's Crump Park, and the following weekend they went to Memphis and split a four-game series with the Red Sox. Their first home game was against the Cleveland Cubs on May 6. By the anxiously awaited July Fourth weekend, the Monarch were 33–7, pitting them as pennant rivals of the well-known Chicago American Giants, whose record was 30–9. They had faced worthy opponents on the roster of prestigious teams, such as the Atlanta Black Crackers, Memphis Red Sox, Birmingham Black Barons, Montgomery Grey Sox, Indianapolis ABCs, the Nashville Elite Giants, the Louisville Black Caps, and the Little Rock Greys.

But that was the past; the future of the pennant race was about to begin. Saturday, July 2, was filled with anticipation and anxiety. Crowds of black and white fans eagerly filled the segregated grandstand seats in Casino Park stadium to watch the talented players on the field. The Monroe Monarchs had stepped up training and player procurement and had as good a claim to the national baseball championship of black America as any other team. But they faced star players on the Pittsburgh Crawfords, including Josh Gibson, Satchel Paige, William Julius "Judy" Johnson, and Ted Radcliffe. They were also big draws to local fans. At this point the Monarchs' chance to get to the playoffs lay in beating the Memphis Red Sox in the July Fourth five-game series. Memphis had a strong team, with eight left-handed batters. This would play to their advantage at Monroe's Casino Park, which had a short right-field wall of only 330 feet.

The grandstand was full to capacity, even the section partitioned off for white folks. Many others were crowding around outside the ballpark listening to the game with or without radios, hoping to be part of the excitement on the field. Things started off badly for the Monarchs. They were quickly caught off guard as the Red Sox scored three runs in the first inning. As frustration mounted, players and fans alike were fearful of a loss. But the Monarchs rallied, and by the fourth inning the score was tied. In the bottom of the eleventh inning, with a 5–5 score, the Monarchs were at bat. The crowd hushed, breaths were held, and hearts nearly stopped. There was one man on third base, but two outs were already on the scoreboard when Monarch Barney Morris got up to bat. Barney eyed his teammate on third and vowed to bring him home. Barney swung with all his might and managed to hit a single. The crowd roared—it was enough to bring the runner on third across home plate. The Monarchs' hopes for a pennant were still alive. Doubleheaders were scheduled for Sunday and Monday, so there was still a lot of work to be done to gain a trip to the World Series.

Rain clouds had rolled in to the Monroe area by the end of the day, and soon the downpour came. It rained and rained. The doubleheader on Sunday, July 3, began with great expectations, but the incessant rain had destroyed the field and the game was called after seven innings. But local enthusiasm was still high; the Monarchs had won the mud-shortened game 5–3. When the remaining game that day was can-celled, the Monarchs felt their chances for the pennant race increase.

For Monroe black residents, the baseball games on Monday, July 4, were the only scheduled activities, and the Monarchs made the day one of celebration for the fans. The Monarchs won the doubleheader 6–1 and 8–2. They were first-half season champions and would go to the playoffs.

The games over the Fourth of July weekend were supposed to have ended the first half of the season, but the *Monroe News-Star* reported that, by the order of the president of the Negro Southern League, in order to determine the winner of the first half of the sea-son, the Monarchs would have to play the Memphis Red Sox again to make up for the rained-out game. Undaunted, Monarchs fans crossed their fingers, whispered beseeching prayers, and once again trusted in the talent of their ball players. This time the game would be played at the white stadium—Forsythe Park—and the only stadium with artificial lighting. The game was scheduled, but no game records, newspaper coverage, or other archival data of the game exist today. It seems the Monarchs won the game because records do exist of the Monarchs playing the Pittsburgh Crawfords in what would be called the 1932 Negro World Series game.

History was made during that July Fourth baseball series. The men of the 1932 Monroe Monarchs team would become the only World Series team that Louisiana would ever field, and its right-handed pitcher Hilton Smith, who joined the Monarchs from the Austin Texas Black Senators for the 1932 season, would be inducted into Baseball's Hall of Fame.

There was much controversy at this time as baseball struggled to survive in a depressed economy. The championship of the Negro

Southern League was disputed, with just percentage points separating the Chicago American Giants and the Monroe Monarchs. No playoff was held. League officials awarded the National Championship to the Chicago American Giants, knowing more people would pay to see a Chicago team than an almost unknown outfit from rural Louisiana, where travel to and from the area was difficult and expensive. The Monarchs played a postseason series in early September with the independent Pittsburgh Crawfords, losing five games to one. This was referred to as a Negro World Series by both teams, but is not considered so by Negro League historians and researchers. The Chicago American Giants, considered by the League to have won the NSL championship, and the Detroit Wolves, who won the East-West League title that year, did not engage in any postseason series. Despite their winning success and support from black newspapers, the Monarchs were excluded from the Negro Southern League when it was reorganized for 1933. The team continued to play in the minor leagues and disbanded soon after 1935; in 1937 Casino Park was leased to a local white team, the Monroe Twins, which became the Monroe White Sox in 1938, playing in the Cotton States League.

But much had been gained by the baseball season of 1932. As their team won national recognition and increased media attention, crime decreased in the community, a black newspaper was established, and white dailies began to carry more news of black sports coverage in general. Today the area that was Casino Park, at South 29 and DeSiard Streets, is a residential area near Carroll High School. But the glory days of America's favorite pastime in Monroe, Louisiana, are not forgotten. The Monroe Monarchs Historical Commission, created in 2005, remembers the heroes of the 1932 Monarchs baseball season and works to build awareness of the historic team and raise money to support local little leagues. The city of Monroe has erected a historical marker in honor of the Monroe Monarchs.

THEY GOT WHAT THEY
HAD COMING

1934

May 23, 1934, began as just another day for the infamous duo. They had been on the run for a while, but had high hopes for a little rest and relaxation soon. Springing Eastham Prison Farm inmates Raymond Hamilton and Henry Methvin back in January had enabled Clyde to exact his revenge on the notorious Texas facility where he had once spent so many tortured days. But the subsequent killing of a guard and the negative publicity meant they were now being hunted like dogs, relentlessly.

Captain Frank A. Hamer, a former Texas Ranger, was assigned by the Texas Department of Corrections to pursue the Barrow Gang. Since February, the tall, stoic law-seeker had often lived out of his car as he stealthily tracked his prey, town after town, always a constant shadow trailing the criminals who continued stealing, bank robbing, and killing. Bonnie still suffered from third-degree leg burns she incurred when the getaway car flipped and caught on fire while the gang was trying to escape toward the Texas–Oklahoma border.

Bonnie Parker, a twenty-three-year-old who had won top honors in school, and Clyde Barrow, a twenty-five-year-old Texas killer, were still under indictment for the January 1933 killing of Tarrant County Deputy Malcolm Davis, and warrants were out for their arrest on February 10, 1934.

The summer had swept in hot and heavy as usual, but times would get even hotter for the wanted criminals. It seemed law enforcement had finally had enough of the murder and mayhem left in the wake of the Barrow Gang. Because of their new notoriety, the necessities of everyday living became problematic. Restaurants and motels loomed as possible ambush sites. Rough campsites, close quarters, and living out of their cars pitted gang members against each other. It was time to split up and as the summer heat turned up full blast, Bonnie and Clyde found themselves on their own. Clyde nursed Bonnie's burns, which had caused the muscles in her right leg to contract and draw up. She could hardly walk and was relegated to hopping on her good leg or being carried from place to place by Clyde. The couple had already made history, but not in a good way, and both were in need of some peace.

Hamer was ever at their back. He had studied the gang's movements, and he knew that they liked to stay close to state borders and put into their getaway plans the "state line" rule that didn't allow officers from one jurisdiction to pursue a fugitive across the border. Hamer knew also that the gang's travel routes often included homes and farms of family members as possible hideout locations. As he tracked the pair to Louisiana, Hamer reckoned the gang was due to drop in on Henry Methvin's family. The law enforcement contingent that he directed included Dallas County Sheriff deputies Bon Alcorn and Ted Hinton, the former Texas Ranger B. M. "Manny" Gault, and Bienville Parish Sheriff Henderson Jordan and his deputy Prentiss Oakley. The posse headed for Louisiana State Highway 154 in

Bienville Parish, in the piney woods of northern Louisiana. They set up an ambush behind an earthen embankment at the top of a small hill where the overgrown brush and trees would keep them hidden. On this desolate road, south of Gibsland toward Sailes, they waited. Each of the six officers had a shotgun and an automatic rifle, as well as pistols.

Bonnie and Clyde had driven their stolen Ford into Gibsland early in the day. They had plans to meet up with Henry Methvin, who had been hiding out at his family's home. First they needed some food. The couple stopped at Ma Canfield's Café and ordered some sandwiches. But Clyde's sixth sense kicked in when he spotted a police car. He decided to bag the sandwiches and eat them on the road. By 8:30 a.m., Bonnie and Clyde were headed south toward the Methvin farm. Barrow was traveling at high speed as he passed the crouching lookout officer who signaled to the hidden posse that it was the infamous duo they were waiting for. Up ahead, Clyde could see old man Methvin's log truck stopped on the road. When he slowed down to see if the man needed help, Clyde suddenly noticed a movement on the opposite side of the road and as he turned his face, the officers were shooting. It was approximately 9:15 a.m., and Bonnie and Clyde had traveled only eight miles from the café.

Deputy Oakley opened fire with his automatic rifle first and then, within seconds, a barrage of bullets hit the car. Clyde's foot slipped off the brake as eight bullets tore through his spinal column; Bonnie's red hat was thrown into the back seat by the force of bullets to the left side of her face. The officers emptied their shotguns next and then grabbed their pistols. So much smoke was coming from the car that it appeared to be on fire. The officers didn't stop shooting even after the car had rolled into the ditch. They didn't want to take any chances. In the spectacular volley, more than 130 rounds of ammunition were pumped into the car; fifty rounds hit their targets.

Barrow was hit in the head, neck, and torso and killed instantly; his body was found hanging lifelessly through the steering wheel. Officers could hear Parker screaming as she was shot. Her body was found against the door, bullets had blown off her right hand, but her left hand still held tightly to a pack of cigarettes. She was found still sitting up with a gun across her lap.

The bullet-ridden stolen car was towed to the small town of Arcadia. The corpses were removed and placed in the rear room of Conger's Furniture on Railroad Avenue, which also served as a funeral parlor. The Bienville Parish coroner was called in for autopsies. Undertaker C. F. "Boots" Bailey complained that the bodies were so riddled with bullet holes they wouldn't hold the embalming fluid.

Items found in the car included stolen automatic rifles, sawed-off semiautomatic shotguns, assorted handguns and pistols, nearly three thousand rounds of ammunition, and license plates from Illinois, Missouri, Texas, Indiana, Kansas, Ohio, Iowa, and Louisiana. Personal effects were there as well: Clyde's sunglasses, a map of Louisiana, Bonnie's makeup, a detective magazine, Clyde's saxophone, and the partly eaten sandwiches.

Thrill seekers from miles around flooded the area almost immediately. Souvenir hunters cut off pieces of Bonnie's dress and locks of her bloody hair. Others collected shards of glass from the car, shell casings, and ripped shreds from Clyde's clothes. Some say that Methvin's father was trying to warn Bonnie and Clyde of the ambush when he stopped his car along the road; others say that his role was part of a bargain to save his son in exchange for helping to bring down Bonnie and Clyde. Whatever the scenario, it was the end of an era. Bonnie, the criminal diva, portrayed as a machine-gun-wielding, chain-smoking killer with a taste for fast times and an occasional cigar, and Clyde, a Robin Hood figure for Depression-era folks who felt powerless in the face of greedy speculators and bank foreclosures, were no more.

Postscripts: Ironically, H. D. Darby, from a nearby town, who had been kidnapped by the Barrow gang the previous year, was brought in to identify the bodies. While he had been held, Bonnie had asked Darby his profession. He had answered that he was an undertaker. She laughingly remarked that someday he may be working on her body. As fate would have it, Darby helped with the embalming of the outlaws.

Henry Barrow was notified of his son's death, and after seeing the body, sat in a rocking chair in the Conger Furniture store and wept.

When she died, Bonnie was wearing her wedding ring from her rocky marriage at age sixteen to Roy Thornton. She was never divorced, although she hadn't seen him in years. He was killed by prison guards on October 3, 1937, while trying to escape from Eastham Farm prison.

Bonnie and Clyde wanted to be buried together, but Bonnie was buried at Crown Hill Memorial Park and Clyde rests in Western Heights Cemetery.

The ambush of Barrow and Parker proved to be the beginning of the end of the "public enemy era" of the 1930s. Bank robbery and kidnapping became federal offenses, the FBI worked more with local jurisdictions, and two-way police car radios made the free-ranging outlaw-bandit lifestyle much more difficult.

The owner of the car Clyde stole and drove to his death got the car back in August 1934, covered with blood, and with an $85 towing and storage bill.

Bonnie and Clyde's story was made into a movie by the same name in 1967 starring Warren Beatty and Faye Dunaway. Estelle Parsons won the Academy Award for best supporting actress for her portrayal of Blanche Barrow.

Prentiss Oakley, who all six lawmen agree fired the first shots, was the only posse member to express regret publicly. He would succeed Henderson Jordan as Bienville Parish sheriff in 1940.

The Bonnie and Clyde Ambush Museum in Gibsland is housed in the former Ma Canfield's Café. Film taken by Ted Hinton with a 16 mm, black-and-white hand-cranked movie camera just after the ambush shows gun smoke still visible around the vehicle.

A stone marker, weathered and defaced by vandals, sits at the site of the Louisiana shoot-out and reads, "On this site May 23, 1934 Clyde Barrow and Bonnie Parker were killed by Law Enforcement Officers. Erected by Bienville Parish Police Jury."

The violent deaths of outlaws Bonnie and Clyde are remembered each year with a festival.

THE KING IS DEAD

1935

Huey Long was rightfully concerned about his safety. He looked around to make sure the six armed guards he had commissioned from the Louisiana State Police were close at hand. His enemies were outraged at the control he still wielded over state government. Rumors of assassination plots were rampant. He had already faced death threats, arson attempts, and a drive-by shooting at his home in New Orleans. Only a couple of months earlier, he had discovered an assassination plot against him when one of his associates reported on a secret meeting of an "assassination club" in New Orleans, attended by four Louisiana congressmen, New Orleans Mayor Walmsley, former Governors Parker and Sanders, and Dr. Carl Weiss (sometimes spelled Wise), a man whose name would soon be etched in the annals of Louisiana history. Others in attendance at the meeting included doctors, attorneys, businessmen, and sundry upper-class citizens who opposed Huey's ideas to bring the people of his state out of illiteracy and poverty.

Huey Pierce Long Jr. had come a long way. Born on August 30, 1893, in Winnfield, a small rural community in the piney woods of north-central Louisiana, he had already beaten the odds against his success. Growing up in one of the poorest parishes in the state in a large, close-knit farming family collided with the oppressive social conditions that existed in 1920 Louisiana. Growing up as the seventh of nine children, he decided early on to champion the common man. He was bright and energetic, skipped the seventh grade, and then failed to graduate because he opposed the addition of a mandatory twelfth year of schooling. Huey won a scholarship to Louisiana State University in a statewide debating competition, but because he couldn't afford textbooks, room, or board, he became a traveling salesman at seventeen, touting the benefits of cooking oil, canned goods, and patent medicines.

He was a successful salesman, married, and seemed headed for a prosperous future. When sales opportunities in a faltering economy dried up, he took up law. At the age of twenty-one, less than a year into the three-year program at Tulane Law School in New Orleans, Huey petitioned to take the bar exam and passed. He returned to Winnfield to practice law, never having earned a single educational diploma. Providing free education to all children would later become a legacy of his political career.

In 1918 he was elected state railroad commissioner for the northern district of Louisiana and in 1922 became chairman of the Public Services Commission (the new name for the Louisiana Railroad Commission) and successfully advocated for lower telephone, gas, and electric rates and railroad and streetcar fares. Huey balked against the ruling hierarchy and sought to replace long-standing cronies with his own supporters, gaining control of the Hospital Board, the Highway Commission, the Levee Board, and the Dock Board. By this time he was the father of a daughter and two sons.

He won the governor's race in 1928 on the platform of public education and social reform. Louisiana's illiteracy rate of 22 percent was the highest in the country—only one in four adults could read, and only half of Louisiana's school-aged children attended school. His cry that "Everyman is a king" resonated through the land, and he won the election by the largest margin in the state's history: 92,941 votes to 3,733. His closest opponent refused to face him in a runoff. At Huey's inauguration, more than fifteen thousand supporters flocked to the capital to see one of their own take the oath as governor.

Huey's commitment to a political agenda of social reform and change was a lightning bolt to a corrupt, elite political system. As governor he built roads and bridges, made free school books available, improved public education and healthcare, and fought for the voting rights of all citizens. His run-ins with the entrenched political stalwarts and the Ku Klux Klan became common stories in the daily newspapers.

When the Great Depression of 1929 rolled in, he was more determined than ever to champion the common man. He felt he could do more in Washington, D.C., and so in 1930, he sought and won a U.S. Senate seat. He hoped his "Share Our Wealth" program would be the cure for the country's ailing economy and a beacon of hope for the disenfranchised masses. He left his old friend, Alvin King, president of the state senate, to act as governor while he was away.

Though he might have been fearful as he neared the capitol in Baton Rouge, the man called "Kingfish" was undaunted in his mission this day, September 8, 1935. Huey excitedly climbed the steps of the Louisiana State Capitol and looked out over the twenty-seven acres of formal gardens and landscape and toward the Mississippi River. He was proud to think that he had made the beautiful and modern state capitol a reality. Just four years earlier, while governor, he had convinced the legislature that a new, efficient building would save the state money. To get the go-ahead to build a large public edifice during the years of the Great Depression was a hard sell, but Huey was confident—after all, he had been a very successful salesman. He reminisced how when the first vote fell four votes short of the two-thirds majority needed, he went into action. While the Speaker of the House ordered a roll call vote, he quickly circulated through the legislative chamber, encouraging a few more supporters to vote in favor of his building. The vote passed. The 450-foot, tallest state capitol in the United States was completed in fourteen months for only $5 million. This price tag included limestone for the exterior and Vermont and Italian marble for the interior.

The grand stairway now before him led up to the fifty-foot entrance door of the art deco capitol. He wasn't aware yet that this would be the last staircase he would walk up or down. U.S. Senator Huey Long was in Baton Rouge for a special session of the Louisiana legislature. A number of bills were before the legislature, including a measure to gerrymander one of Long's opponents, Judge Benjamin Pavy, out of office. Huey was there to throw his support behind this bill. His friend and ally, Oscar K. (O. K.) Allen was governor. Some say he was just Huey's puppet and that Huey was still in control. Just two months before, Long had announced his candidacy for the 1936 presidency and was basking in the light of a bright political future.

Long stepped confidently through the large doors of his beloved capitol and entered Memorial Hall. It felt like home as he took purposeful strides to his meeting in the governor's office. When he emerged back into the corridor with Supreme Court justice John Fournet at his side, his bodyguards quickly surrounded him, but trouble was lurking. Fournet first noticed the strange look on Huey's face, and then spied a flourished .32 automatic gun. A flurry of panicked activity ensued. Gunshots rang out explosively.

The actual details of that day are still debated. The generally accepted version is that Judge Pavy's son-in-law, Dr. Carl Weiss, who had been at the "assassination club" meeting, was upset at Long's appearance in the capitol to oust Pavy. Weiss approached Huey in the corridor and shot him at close range in the abdomen. Huey's bodyguards immediately opened fire on Weiss. Others report that Weiss had only taken a swing with his fist at Long and, in the melee, a bullet from one of Long's bodyguards ricocheted off the marble pillar and hit Huey in the lower spine.

In either case, the capitol was rife with bullets from the flurry of shots, and today the pockmarks are still evident. The corridor filled with smoke as Huey staggered down the hallway, grasping his side with his right hand. He descended the grand stairway, was helped into a car, and taken to the nearby Our Lady of the Lake sanitarium.

Weiss was killed instantly. The number of shots fired is not known. Thirty bullet wounds were found on the front side of Weiss' body, twenty-nine on the back, and two bullet wounds were found in his head. It was impossible to determine how many wounds were caused by the same bullet entering and exiting.

At the new four-story medical facility run by the Franciscan Missionaries of Our Lady, it was determined that surgery was necessary to repair the bullet hole in Long's abdomen. A call was sent out to two of the finest surgeons in New Orleans to get to Baton Rouge immediately to perform the operation.

In 1928, Louisiana had only 331 miles of paved roads and Huey had launched an infrastructure program to construct three thousand miles of roads. Ironically, one of Huey's pet roadwork projects, a new eighty-mile concrete Airline Highway to connect New Orleans and Baton Rouge was under construction at the time of the shooting. The New Orleans surgeons were forced to take the old River Road, a lengthy, twisting road along the bank of the Mississippi River. As fate would have it that tragic day, they had a car accident along the way. Dr. Arthur Vidrine, the attending physician, would have to perform the surgery. During the two-hour operation, Dr. Vidrine repaired two small wounds in the colon and abdomen. When the two surgeons finally arrived from New Orleans, they determined that one of Long's kidneys had also been injured. Surgery was imperative, but by this time Long was too weak to survive another operation.

Long's family was also en route to Baton Rouge from New Orleans. They took the new highway despite the construction hazards, his two teenage sons removing barricades as they raced to their father's side. By his bedside Long's sister, Lucille, repeated the Kingfish's plea, "God, don't let me die! I have so much to do!" At 4:06 a.m., on September 10, Huey Long died of internal bleeding at the age of forty-two. His book, *My First Days in the White House*, was published posthumously. His widow, Rose, was appointed to fill Huey's seat in the Senate and was later elected to the position, making her the second woman elected to the U.S. Senate.

Huey's death made news headlines around the world, and more than two hundred thousand mourners, eight times the city's population, traveled to Baton Rouge to pay their respects. Long's casket was carried down the steps of the Louisiana State Capitol, and the Rev. Gerald Smith led the procession to Long's interment on the grounds of the State Capitol he had built. Long is now immortalized by statues at the Louisiana State Capitol and the U.S. Capitol.

BOMBING WITH SACKS OF FLOUR

1941

After Poland was overrun by Germany's armored columns, Hitler was poised to strike France and it seemed inevitable that the United States would enter the war in Europe. America's military leaders had to prepare the United States for battle. In September 1939, Congress mobilized the National Guard and Reserve and had voted to substantially increase the size of the Army. The U.S. military was primarily an infantry force, but with war looming, military leaders needed to quickly find the best ways to train soldiers to use newer, more mechanized weapons. No field maneuver exercises had been conducted by the Army since World War I, and commanders knew they would have to update an untrained military on modern tactical warfare. It was time for action. It was past time for action!

Army Chief of Staff General George C. Marshall was determined to implement a rigorous training program. He put forth his military plans in a "Protective Mobilization Plan" that President Franklin D. Roosevelt signed on September 8, 1939. Marshall called on Lt. Gen. Stanley D. Embick and Colonel Mark Wayne Clark to find an area large enough to accommodate the numbers of troops scheduled to be trained in a series of maneuvers that would test their readiness. Armed with these instructions the two men almost immediately looked toward the Kisatchie National Forest's 604,000-acre pine-wood wilderness and thousands of surrounding acres of unused land in central and northern Louisiana. By early June 1940, the Army had secured the right to deploy troops across thousands of square miles in the Grant, Natchitoches, Winn, Rapides, Vernon, Claiborne, and Webster Parishes in Louisiana. The sparsely populated back country of winding roads, swampy terrain, and dense forest was perfect and quickly became the site of several large military bases and training camps. Within a short time the area was home to camps Claiborne, Livingston, Polk, and Beauregard, and army air fields in Lake Charles, DeRidder, Alexandria, Pineville, and Pollack.

By August 1941, the camps and training facilities were in full operation and trained military teams from various camps were ready to engage in what would be called the Louisiana Maneuvers, a series of training exercises that would rigorously test the skills and expertise of U.S. military men. Marshall appointed General Leslie McNair as Army director, with the directive that tactical errors should happen in the fields of Louisiana, not on the battlefields of Europe.

The maneuvers would be a good opportunity to test the Army's new halftrack-mounted 75 mm antitank gun as well as to find out if mobile units could adequately replace horse cavalry. Other questions revolved around the operation of newly formed paratrooper units, the maneuverability of armored vehicles in difficult terrain and harsh weather conditions, and the ability of U.S. officers to command multiple units over large areas.

The Louisiana Maneuvers were headquartered at Camp Polk (later Fort Polk) and would take place on 3,400 square miles of land stretching east from the Sabine River to the Calcasieu River and north to the

Red River. These exercises, called simply "maneuvers," would take place until 1944. Troops were billeted at the various camps in seemingly endless lines of pup tents. In the field they camped out in densely wooded areas; some found shelter in local barns. The troops crossed rivers and sloshed through murky swamps while shooting at each other with wooden rifles. Flour sack bombs, dropped by dive bombers, were dodged as units maneuvered for victory. Officers insisted the maneuvers be as realistic as possible. Loudspeakers blared out recorded sounds of battle while smoke from canisters floated out over the battlefield and aircraft dropped bags of sand to simulate the impact of artillery shells. Millions of rounds of blank ammunition were allotted to soldiers, and rules governing engagement and "casualties" were established. Battles took place on lawns, in private yards, on town streets, and in the surrounding forests. Truces were declared at lunchtime so that the soldiers could eat. Hundreds of "umpires," armed with clipboards and armbands, assessed units and leaders according to a complex grading system and ruled on how many soldiers were "killed or injured." Monitoring the time it took medical units to transfer the "wounded" to combat hospitals was also important.

The rural citizens could not believe the number of troops training in their area and told countless stories of men and tanks rumbling through their quiet villages. They reported being stuck in places, unable to get home, while battles were fought in city streets, and remembered soldiers trying to get additional corn for their horses from fields and corncribs. They were awed by the stately cavalry horses and stubborn Missouri mules used to pull field artillery. Soon, these cavalry mounts would be exchanged for motor vehicles and scout cars. They also spoke highly of the great leaders who frequented their restaurants and other establishments.

In September 1941, just three months before the bombing of Pearl Harbor, the largest of all maneuvers took place and earned the moniker, "The Big One." Congress, knowing that the country would soon join the war in Europe, allocated $21 million of the Military Allocations Act to the enterprise. Marshall appointed Brigadier General Lesley "Whitey" McNair, commandant of the Army's Command and General Staff School at Fort Leavenworth, Kansas, to lead the largest peacetime exercise in American history. Marshall called the 1941 maneuvers "a combat college for troop leading" and a test of the "new armored, antitank and air forces that had come of age since 1918." McNair's groundbreaking war games mobilized nearly half a million men split into nineteen army divisions. These divisions engaged in a mock battle for "navigation rights" of the Mississippi River as two opposing armies of two fictitious countries. Red Kotmk, representing Kansas, Oklahoma, Texas, Missouri, and Kentucky, and headed by General Ben Lear, would go up against Blue Almat, representing Arkansas, Louisiana, Mississippi, Alabama, and Tennessee, headed by General Walter Krueger, a veteran taskmaster, and his Chief of Staff, Colonel Dwight D. Eisenhower. The exercises were made up of two phases: three weeks in August and three weeks in September. Lear's Red Army would try to take Louisiana from the Blue Army, which was occupying the area. Lear called upon Patton to lead a lightning strike against Krueger's Louisiana's defenses. Krueger's Blue Army mobile corps managed to pin the Red Army, with Patton's tanks in the lead, against the river, despite Patton's offer to pay $50 to any man who could capture "a certain SOB called Eisenhower." Umpires agreed the flanking maneuver was successful and awarded the Blue Army, under Eisenhower's leadership, the win. Because of this win, Marshall would add Eisenhower's name to the list of future military leaders that already included Bradley, Stilwell, Clark, and Patton. Eisenhower would later be promoted to brigadier general and ultimately supreme allied commander. CBS reporter Eric Sevareid commented that Eisenhower "makes more sense than any of the rest of them." Reporter Drew Pearson said that Eisenhower had both "a steel-trap mind plus unusual physical vigor." Armies were shuffled for the next set of battles and in the latter part of September, Patton's 2nd Armored Division advanced two hundred miles through northern Louisiana and East Texas in three days, enveloping Lear's flank in a brilliant maneuver. One story goes that Patton had stalled the advance of Lieutenant General Krueger's entire army by buying up all the gasoline in the area with IOUs. While Marshall had noted Eisenhower's talent, he was also impressed by Patton's aggressiveness on the battlefield. History has recorded the achievements of Patton, Clark, Bradley, and Eisenhower, who brought to Europe the military expertise they had gained in Louisiana.

The mock battles of what became known as the Louisiana Maneuvers had one purpose: to prepare America's soldiers for the war that had already begun in Europe and was threatening to spread around the world. The Louisiana Maneuvers of 1941 proved the usefulness of tanks in modern warfare, and Army planners learned about reconnaissance and troop supply problems that could be encountered on the battlefield.

The troops had to learn to deal with the unique Louisiana environs, which included mosquitoes, the harsh summer climate, humidity, poisonous "chinaberries," coral snakes, ticks, and chiggers. In the World War II movie *A Walk in the Sun*, when soldiers were commanded to storm a farmhouse held by the Germans, one soldier reminds his buddies that as bad as the confrontation might get, "it can't be worse than the Louisiana Maneuvers." Bing Crosby, in a Command Performance radio program on V-J Day in 1945, gave credit to the Louisiana Maneuvers for training the soldiers. It is said that the cavalry horses mixed with the wild horse herd in the area, and their descendants still roam freely today. The only other remnants of the Great Maneuvers are a few foxholes and cartridge castings and remains of old ration cans buried under the Louisiana soil.

FAMOUS P.O.W. GETS A
TASTE OF LOUISIANA

1942

Camp Livingston, an active military training installation from 1940 to 1945, sat deep in the dense yellow pine forests of central Louisiana. Its forty-seven thousand acres spanned the borders of Grant and Rapides Parishes. Here soldiers took part in the notorious Louisiana Maneuvers and trained exhaustively to defend their country. Camp Livingston was originally named Camp Tioga, but its name was changed to honor Robert R. Livingston, negotiator of the Louisiana Purchase. During the war, over five hundred thousand troops trained at Camp Livingston, including the 38th Infantry Division, the "Avengers of Bataan," the 86th Infantry Division, the first U.S. unit to cross the Danube River into Germany, and a distinguished Army Air Corps aviation squad of 250 African Americans.

Camp Livingston was also a designated internment facility and temporary home to thousands of Japanese internees who had been rounded up throughout the United States and Latin America. Detainees were shuffled around the country for years; many arrived in Louisiana from Fort Missoula, the Department of Justice internment camp, and the U.S. Army–run Fort Sill and Camp Forrest internment camps. Many Issei internees from Hawaii were reunited at Camp Livingston.

On June 8, 1942, Camp Livingston became a P.O.W. camp. Emergency wartime regulations stated that P.O.W. camps must not be within 170 miles of a coastline, within 150 miles of a national border, or near shipyards, ammunition plants, or other wartime industries. Camp Livingston fit the bill. The thinking was that these parameters would deter sabotage and escape.

The camp was well liked. Detainees, treated under the guidelines of the Geneva Convention of 1929, reported fair treatment and good food. However, there were endless complaints about the stifling heat and suffocating humidity. Temperatures could reach 130 degrees Fahrenheit in summer. To find relief from the extreme heat, some prisoners dug shallow pits in the dirt under their barracks and rested there during the hottest hours of the day, while others cooled off by spending most of the day stripped down to their underwear. Although the camp commander was strict, some of the only reported "hardships" were the ominous presence of poisonous reptiles, stinging insects, and large fireflies. The Geneva Convention stipulated that prisoners, other than officers, could be required to work as long as that work was not related to the war effort. At Camp Livingston, both P.O.W.s and internees helped to maintain the camp facilities and operations, while others cut down pine trees in the Louisiana forest to build an airport. The great majority worked the tobacco, cotton, and sugarcane fields in the surrounding areas.

Camp Livingston was built to accommodate five thousand men, and so many Japanese, German, and Italian prisoners taken captive during the war were sent south to the piney woods and prairies of Louisiana. Camp Livingston received so many Japanese P.O.W.s that hospital buildings were labeled with Japanese characters. When a new batch of Japanese P.O.W.s arrived at camp, no one paid too much attention . . . until it was discovered who was among that group.

You may not recognize the name, but you will know the story. December 7, 1941, is perhaps one of the most remembered dates in the history of the United States. And one small spot in central Louisiana played a crucial role in that tragic story.

Kazuo Sakamaki was honored to be a crew member of the miniature submarine fleet operated by the Japanese Navy. He had been handpicked for his physical strength, determination to succeed, and fighting spirit. He was unmarried and from a large family, keeping him free from worrying about loved ones depending on his care.

His submarine was one of the five small subs in the Pacific waters around Hawaii that fateful day. Sakamaki's midget sub, armed with two 1,000-pound torpedoes, was launched from a mother submarine ten miles off Pearl Harbor about 11:00 p.m. on December 6. He and the nine other men staffing the boats were following orders as they maneuvered their 78.5-foot mini submarines into position to attack U.S. battleships and destroyers. As all hell broke loose around him in the surprise attack on Pearl Harbor, Sakamaki found that his gyrocompass was malfunctioning. He struggled to get his submarine going in the right direction. The craft eventually hit a coral reef a few miles off the coastline and ran aground. A U.S. Navy destroyer spotted the impaired sub and opened fire. The depth charges caused some damage and, as the sub filled with smoke and fumes from leaking gas, Sakamaki was determined to destroy the Japanese Imperial Navy submarine before it could get into the hands of the enemy. He set the demolition charges, then he and Chief Warrant Officer Kiyoshi Inagaki abandoned the submarine and attempted to swim the seven hundred feet to the shore. Inagaki drowned in the giant waves of the Hawaiian waters, but an exhausted Sakamaki managed to get to shore, where he collapsed unconscious on Waimanalo Beach.

On the morning of December 8, 1941, U.S. Corporal David M. Akui and Lieutenant Paul C. Plybon of Company G, 298th Infantry Regiment of the Hawaiian National Guard, stood above the beached figure. Akui drew his pistol. When he realized the man was Japanese, he took him into custody. Sakamaki put up no resistance. Twenty-one-year-old Akui became famous for capturing of the first Japanese prisoner of war in World War II.

The prisoner awoke in a hospital bed under armed guard and was identified as Ensign Kazuo Sakamaki, commander of a two-man midget submarine. As a Special Attack Force member, Sakamaki was on a suicide mission; he had no expectation of coming back alive. Shamed by his failure to attack U.S. boats, abandoning his submarine, and being captured, Sakamaki requested to be allowed to commit suicide. His many requests were routinely denied. The demolition charges had failed and his submarine was washed ashore and taken into U.S. custody. Sakamaki was first sent to Fort Shafter near Honolulu for questioning, and then he was routed to Camp Livingston in Louisiana. Sakamaki's submarine was salvaged, cleaned, and shipped to the United States for a 1942 War Bond tour.

It is not reported how long Sakamaki stayed at Camp Livingston, but his memoir mentions the kindness of Lieutenant Colonel Dan, commander of the camp, and others in charge there. He also valued the educational opportunities provided at the camp's "Interment University" run by the Reverend Kano, a Japanese Episcopal clergyman. He attended lectures on geography, commerce, agriculture, Japanese poetry, and music. He encouraged other Japanese P.O.W.s to learn English and tried to help those who felt suicide was the only answer to the shame they faced. At Camp Livingston, the P.O.W.s and the internees (calling themselves "State Guests") were allowed to mix recreationally. Softball games were a popular pastime. A P.O.W. cemetery was located on Camp Livingston grounds.

In late 1945, Camp Livingston was deactivated and is now part of the Kisatchie National Forest and under the jurisdiction of the U.S. Forest Service. In 1947 the headstones from the P.O.W. cemetery were relocated to Fort Sam Houston in Texas. There is not much left today, just remnants left behind of the glory that was once Camp Livingston. Some of the old paved streets remain and can still be driven down in a car; some are used daily by traffic passing through the camp grounds. The footings of many buildings are visible and a run-down building called Therapy Ward can be seen. Two swimming pools also remain. Most recent maps put the locations of the P.O.W. camps in Area 20, near the all-terrain vehicle (ATV) trailhead. The U.S. Forest Service maintains the Little Creek and Hickman Trails for multiple-use, including ATVs. Artwork and storytelling graffiti, said to have been created by Italian P.O.W.s, have been discovered on crumbling concrete prison walls still visible in the complex area.

Sakamaki's submarine is now in the Admiral Nimitz Museum in Fredericksburg, Texas. In 1991, Sakamaki wept openly when he visited the museum to view his midget submarine that had been captured fifty years earlier. A retiree of the Toyota Motor Co., Sakamaki passed away in 1999; he was eighty-one years old, but in his youth he had once tasted Louisiana's southern hospitality.

DEAD WOMAN WALKING

1942

Long before the 1995 movie *Dead Man Walking*, in which Sister Helen Prejean (played by Susan Sarandon) acts as spiritual advisor for Matthew Poncelet, a murderer on death row in Louisiana (played by Sean Penn), a woman was executed in Louisiana's electric chair . . . the only one on record.

By sixteen, pretty and petite Toni Jo was a familiar figure in the seedy underworld of Shreveport, Louisiana. Because she was a juvenile, she had so far managed to avoid prison for her illegal activities, including assault. At thirteen, she left her abusive home to work in a macaroni factory. She was fired when the manager found that her mother had died of dreaded tuberculosis. Toni Jo, with only a sixth-grade education, turned to prostitution as a way to support herself. In 1939, she was working in a brothel in Shreveport's "red light district" and was addicted to cocaine when she fell in love with Claude David "Cowboy" Henry, a down-on-his-luck prizefighter.

The two married on November 25, 1939, in Shreveport; Toni Jo used her real name, Annie Beatrice McQuiston. The couple honeymooned in southern California. When exactly Cowboy shared the fact that he was out on bail for shooting a Texas ex–police officer with his new bride is unknown. But while honeymooning, Cowboy received a telegram to appear in a Texas court. Toni Jo pleaded with Cowboy to go "on the run" with her, but he opted to stand trial. Cowboy was convicted and sent to the Texas State Penitentiary in Huntsville, Texas, for fifty years.

Toni Jo, convinced that her husband had acted in self-defense, had expected his acquittal. When the jury returned a "guilty" charge, Toni Jo vowed to get him out of jail. She moved to Beaumont, Texas, to be near Cowboy and befriended Harold "Arkie" (shortened from Arkansas) Burks, a young man who would become her accomplice. Arkie, absent without leave from the army, had previously served a sentence in the Huntsville penitentiary and had the inside information she needed. The pair decided robbing a bank would be the best way to get the money they needed to cover their expenses. But first they needed a car. To that end, Toni Jo convinced one of her criminal acquaintances to steal some pistols from a gun shop for them. Armed with the weapons and posing as newlyweds, the duo hitchhiked toward the Arkansas bank that Arkie said would be the best to knock over. They got as far as Orange, Texas, when the "right" car came along. The new Ford V8 Coupe was perfect! Fast for its day, it might be capable of outrunning the police.

Joseph P. Calloway was delivering the Ford for a friend in Jennings, Louisiana, when he happened upon Toni Jo and Arkie. Perhaps because it was Valentine's Day, Calloway offered the couple a ride. They passed through Lake Charles without any hint of trouble, but once they were out in the country, Toni Jo pulled out a .32 caliber revolver and demanded Calloway turn off the main highway and stop the car. They got out and commanded Calloway to remove all his clothes. Arkie gathered them in a bundle along with Calloway's watch and $15. Toni Jo wanted the clothes for Cowboy to change into. They drove off with Calloway in the trunk. At an empty pasture, they stopped and ordered Calloway out of the trunk at gunpoint, forcing him to kneel behind some tall haystacks. Toni Jo suggested he say his prayers. Calloway died with a .32 caliber bullet in his head.

Toni Jo and Arkie continued driving the Ford through the night to Camden, Arkansas, and checked into a cheap hotel. Arkie had second thoughts about the killing and, grabbing the bundle of Calloway's clothes, fled. Toni Jo used the stolen money for a bus ticket back to Shreveport and showed up at her aunt's house. When she realized Toni Jo was in trouble, her aunt called in a family friend, Sgt. Dave Walker. Walker was not prepared for Toni Jo's confession, much less her submission of the revolver with one fired and five live rounds in it. Walker handed Toni Jo over to the Lake Charles police. She directed them to the exact spot where Calloway's body lay covered with straw. The fatal bullet matched Toni Jo's gun. The Ford coupe, discovered in Arkansas where Arkie had abandoned it, contained Calloway's clothing and cigarette butts with lipstick on them. Toni Jo was charged with murder. She revealed her accomplice and Arkie was soon arrested and charged with murder, too.

Toni Jo's first trial began March 27, 1940. The trial attracted a lot of press coverage due in part to Toni Jo's sultry good looks. Toni Jo adamantly claimed Arkie had shot Calloway. The jury didn't buy Toni Jo's story and after deliberating for six hours, unanimously found her guilty, sentencing her to death by hanging. Toni Jo displayed no emotion when the verdict was read. Arkie was also convicted and sentenced to death.

Toni Jo appealed. During the new trial, Arkie denied Toni Jo's charge that he had fired the fatal shot. This time, the jury deliberated only one hour before convicting Toni Jo and again sentencing her to death.

Toni Jo appealed and won a third trial. In January 1942, Toni Jo was once again convicted and sentenced to death. Since her first sentencing two years earlier, hanging was no longer used in Louisiana. The new method of execution was death by the electric chair. Toni Jo appealed yet again, this time, however, she was denied. In Lake Charles prison she met Father Wayne Richard, a local Catholic priest, who listened to the confessions of a young woman who had never gotten over her mother's death, been beaten by her father, begged her aunt to take her away from her wretched home life, and left home at thirteen.

On November 23, 1942, just five days before his wife's execution, Cowboy broke out of prison to see her one last time. Cowboy was recaptured in Beaumont, Texas, just a few miles from the Louisiana border.

When Toni Jo was given a last wish, she wanted to phone Cowboy. In the jailer's office, a cheerful Toni Jo told Cowboy, "I am ready for it." Then she pleaded with Cowboy to make something of his life. He was crying by the end of the conversation.

Toni Jo had trouble sleeping that night and admitted to a sheriff's deputy that she felt "scared inside."

Toni Jo's electrocution was set for Saturday, November 28, 1942, at 12:05 p.m. She enjoyed the company of a small black-and-white dog in her last hours, and then slipped on a plain black dress and black pumps. She posed for pictures, broadly smiling for the cameras. But reality hit soon enough, and Toni Jo cried when her head was shaved. She requested a brightly colored scarf, and one was found for her.

Toni Jo would be executed in the basement of the prison. Gertie, a portable electric chair, had been transported from Angola, Louisiana's notorious state penitentiary, the previous day. Deputy Sheriff Kenny Reid read her death warrant and asked Toni Jo if she had a final statement. She replied, "I think not." The twenty-six-year-old convicted murderer held Father Richard's hand as he led her down the stairs to the execution chamber. She was allowed to pray for a few moments. Toni Jo flashed a smile at her executioner and mumbled a few inaudible words as she was strapped into the chair. Electrodes were applied to her shaven scalp and legs and a leather mask was put over her face. Moments later, two thousand volts surged through Toni Jo's young body and at 12:12 p.m. the prison doctor declared her dead. Her body was removed moments later. Father Richard officiated at Toni Jo's burial in Orange Grove Cemetery. Her last request was to hold a crucifix in her hand.

Toni Jo's was the sixth electrocution carried out in the state. Arkie was executed in the same electric chair on March 23, 1943, despite Toni Jo's confession. No relatives claimed his body. On July 15, 1945, on parole because of ill health, Cowboy was killed in Dallas.

Capital punishment is legal in Louisiana and while more than seven hundred men have been executed in Louisiana, only one woman, Toni Jo Henry, has achieved that distinction. Gruesome Gertie, the electric chair, was used from 1941 to 1991, and is now on display at the Angola museum. The current and sole method of execution in Louisiana is lethal injection

The Pardon, a 2013 film based on Toni Jo's story, was shot on location in Shreveport.

HEEL STRING GANG MAKES
THEIR DEMANDS HEARD

1951

The 1950s was one of the most notorious protest eras in the U.S. penal system. But as the worst cruelties of prison life—filthy living conditions, beatings, torture, and starvation—were systematically eliminated from U.S. prisons, there remained one exception. The Louisiana State Penitentiary, the largest maximum security prison in the United States, opened in 1901 and was named Angola, after one of the four plantations that made up the land parcel. It sits on eighteen thousand acres, hidden in a big, looping bend of the Mississippi River. The area is, ironically, shaped like an animal trap, with three sides barricaded by the levees bordering the Mississippi River and the other cut off by the dense undergrowth jaws of the Tunica Hills. The prison houses more than five thousand offenders and eighteen hundred staff members. Angola has the largest number of inmates with life sentences in the United States. In a state where "a life sentence" means life, the average tenure of an Angola inmate is ninety years and few prisoners are paroled before spending fifty years behind bars. The penal complex is called "The Farm" by inmates and "The Alcatraz of the South" by critics. To most locals it is simply the feared "Angola." Prior to 1951, the public knew little about what went on behind the closed doors of the prison. When investigators finally exposed the rule by buckshot, leather strap, and rubber hose, *Collier's Weekly* called the Louisiana State Penitentiary "America's Worst Prison."

Conditions at Angola were harsh and often inhumane; some say the inmates were treated worse than the slaves of an earlier century. Convicts were jammed into foul-smelling barracks and ruled with what *Life Magazine* called a "Beat them to a pulp attitude." In 1952, Warden Henderson was ruling Angola with an iron hand. Unreported flogging was a regular practice. Workers in the sugarcane fields were repeatedly beaten by handpicked, privileged convict overseers on horseback. These men would run down victims and beat them within inches of their lives with hickory sticks if they showed lazy behavior or resistance at the end of their fourteen-hour day, a hard labor sentence that began at "can see" and ended at "can't see." The men were fed 28 cents' worth of food a day and received two black-and-white-striped suits a year, no underwear.

Punishment for failure to follow orders also included prisoners being forced to lay spread-eagle on the ground; while the victim's arms and legs were held out by other convicts, a "prison official" beat him with a leather whip called the "bat." Thirty blows were enough to send a man to the hospital. A small infirmary had been added to the penal complex in 1940 to take care of beaten, sick, or injured prisoners, but it was staffed by only one permanent nurse. No doctor was on-site. Other forms of torture were sweat boxes—tin-roofed, four-foot-square enclosures set up in the fields where prisoners would be confined during the hottest times of the day. Twelve hours spent inside led to heatstroke.

Other prisoners were punished by being handcuffed to whipping posts, where they were beaten and left in the sun to scorch. As an added torture, Epsom salts would be poured into their mouths as they starved nearly to death while tethered to the whipping posts for days.

The "Red Hat Cell Block" was named after the red-painted straw hats that the most dangerous prisoners wore while working in the fields in order to be more visible. These quarters were made up of confinement cells known as Red Hats and were described as a dungeon crawling with rats. Inmates were served dinner in stinking buckets that sloshed out onto the floor.

On February 19, 1951, this was the scene of a gruesome inmate protest. Prisoners sought relief from an extreme substandard existence that included cramped and unsanitary living quarters, slave-like working conditions, lack of clean clothes, and no hot water, all happening under the constant threat of violence and brutality of prison guards, administration, and other prisoners. Records showed that the causes of prisoner deaths included broken backs, accidental shootings, hemorrhage, shock, drowning, and heat exhaustion, but 28 percent of deaths at Angola were of "unknown" or "unlisted" causes.

In a defiant move, inmates managed to obtain razor blades and slash through their heel tendons. Irishwoman Mrs. Mary Margaret Daughtry, Angola's first woman nurse, devotedly served the men of Angola for seven years. She said the first men to slash their heels were Red Hat inmates who had been sentenced to sixty days but who had already been kept in the dungeon for eight months. This self-mutilation made it impossible for them to work the fields. They were dubbed the "Heel String Gang" because they hopped around their barracks in a weird painful dance singing "The Heel String Boogie" in protest. A prisoner reported, "They hauled us over to the hospital—to nurse Mrs. Mary Margaret Daughtry—no doctor then." He also revealed that letters were smuggled out to the Shreveport and New Orleans newspapers to let them know what was going on. The *Shreveport Journal* was the first media outlet to break the story that twenty-seven men had crippled themselves by slitting their left Achilles tendons to attract public attention to the awful conditions. Within days five more men had hamstrung themselves. The plight of the Heel String Gang caused national news organizations to uncover prison conditions and prisoner grievances. On February 26, 1951, now that their left heels were mending, ten men also cut their right heel tendons. One inmate explained "It didn't hurt much, just a little sting, but when that tendon let loose and flew up your leg, you could sure feel that . . ."

Nurse Daughtry described the incident in a statement to the investigating governor-appointed committee of thirty-four citizens, including reporters, judges, peace officers, reformers, and Negro leaders. One reporter on the committee said, "We conducted 'hearings' at Angola in March of 1951 in an almost dreamlike atmosphere of first come first served. For two days we listened to men who were sent before us we know not whence, nor how, nor why." The committee was slow to get any substantial reform, but blue denim cloth for suits was ordered to replace the black and white stripes. Nurse Daughtry quit in protest to the committee's and administration's inaction in April, saying, "There is . . . no trade school, no handicrafts or arts— not even a library. A man sentenced here who cannot read or write leaves here the same way."

Today Angola's inmates have been freed from their former state of fear and dread. The dungeons have been dismantled. Inmates have their own prison magazine, the *Angolite*, and Angola is the only penitentiary in the country with an FCC radio license for its KLSP radio station. The very popular annual Angola Rodeo is attended by thousands of locals, who munch on Cajun food and cheer on prisoners riding bulls and roping calves.

LOUISIANA HAYRIDE JUMP
STARTS A CAREER

1954

In 1954, the *Louisiana Hayride* was one of the most well-known country music programs in the United States. The show began on April 3, 1948, and was broadcast on local radio station KWKH, a fifty-thousand-watt clear station reaching twenty-eight states. Soon it was on the CBS radio network of 198 affiliates across the country and the Armed Forces Radio. The *Hayride* was broadcast from the Municipal Auditorium in Shreveport, a northwestern Louisiana city proud of its rural heritage, racial toleration, and the "star names" it attracted. The grand art deco building, a popular place for concerts, boxing matches, and theater productions, was built in the 1920s to honor the servicemen of World War I. The concert hall, called the "Muni" by locals, housed a 3,800-seat auditorium, and on Saturday nights during the 1950s its seats were filled to capacity when the best-known country stars performed live on its stage. The very first broadcast of the *Hayride* brought in country celebrities Kitty Wells, the Four Deacons, Curley Kinsey and the Tennessee Ridge Runners, and the Mercer Brothers, but unlike its competitor, the *Grand Old Opry*, the *Hayride* also provided a platform for unknown artists. The *Hayride* became known for musical innovation and launched the careers of regulars such as Hank Williams, yodeler Slim Whitman, Jim Reeves, and Johnny Cash. So many musicians got their start on the *Hayride* that it was called "The Cradle of the Stars."

On the evening of October 16, 1954, KWKH radio announcer Frank Page was ready to introduce a nineteen-year-old singer who was struggling to make it big. Calling himself the "Hillbilly Cat," he would have a chance to shine at that night's two performances. The singer had been given a slot on the show because country duet Jimmy (Jimmy Lee Fautheree) and Johnny (Johnny Mathis) wanted out of their agreement to accept a lucrative concert out west. The *Hayride* filled their slot with a new name from Memphis, Tennessee. Page would be the emcee for this portion of the show and it was up to him to build up the performer for the crowd.

After a gig in Memphis, the fledgling star had driven all night with agent Sam Phillips, guitarist Scotty Moore, and bassist Bill Black. They had arrived in town after missing the turnoff in Greenville, Mississippi, and nearly running over a team of mules on the road. First they checked into the Captain Shreve Hotel in downtown Shreveport, and then began to work the music scene. They visited with "T. Tommie" Cutrer, a local DJ who played the group's music on WCLJ. He said he would help get word out about their concert that night. They also met with the *Hayride*'s booking agent, Pappy Covington, who encouraged the group in their musical pursuits. After a short stop at Stan Lewis's record shop, one of the largest record distributors in the region, they headed to the Muni. The facility looked great. It was bigger than the *Grand Ole Opry*'s Ryman Auditorium, where they had played, disappointedly, just two weeks before. There were large dressing rooms backstage and a great place where performers could visit with each other. And, best of all, the acoustics were great.

Locals flocked to the Muni on Saturday nights and tonight would be no different. The tickets cost 60 cents for adults and 30 cents for children. Audiences were known for their enthusiasm, and the mostly white and older crowd attending the first performance was eager for the show to begin. The producer of the *Hayride*, Horace Logan, flamboyantly approached the microphone in a ten-gallon cowboy hat and six-shooters on his hips. The young performer offstage looked out anxiously at the largest audience he had ever played. After Logan had warmed up the house, the band struck up with its theme, "Raise a Ruckus Tonight." The crowd finished the lyrics: "Come along, everybody come along, while the moon is shining bright, we're going to have a wonderful time at the *Louisiana Hayride* tonight!"

Emcee Page stepped up to the mike and beckoned the singing group onto the stage. The lead singer wore a pink jacket, a black shirt, and two-toned shoes. Moore and Black were in western-style shirts. Page introduced the trio and asked if they were ready to perform. They said yes and added, "We're gonna do a song for ya we got out on Sun Records." The singer seemed nervous, maybe he was even suffering from stage fright, but he was eager to please the audience with his "new kind of act." The crowd didn't like the singer's jerky legs and black rhythm-and-blues style. They didn't appreciate the singer's energy and displayed passion, and the performance fell flat, much as it had at the *Grand Ole Opry* earlier when manager Jim Denny said the act was "not bad" but didn't suit the *Opry*'s program well.

In contrast to the *Opry*, Page described the *Hayride* as "loose as a goose," saying it wanted to showcase all kinds of entertainers and musical styles. Performers were able to choose their own songs and could try out various styles of performing. The more adventurous *Hayride* was an artistic incubator where performers could craft their style and skill while waiting to make it big in Nashville.

The young singer with the strange name decided to try something else for his second performance. During intermission, his agent had advised him to be himself, saying if he didn't loosen up, he would surely fail. Raucous crowds from local universities, Barksdale Air Force Base just across the Red River, and the East Texas music scene packed the main floor and wraparound balconies for the later, second show. A roaring cheer emanated after the first bars of "That's Alright, Mama." The house drummer, D. J. Fontana, had an idea. He began to complement Presley's movements with an accented beat, a technique he had learned while playing in strip joints. The singer finally relaxed, and his unique rock n' roll style took over. When he curled his lip and slurred the lyrics, the crowd roared. When Elvis wiggled his hips, the audience responded, and he shook a little more. As Elvis began to gyrate more dramatically, the young people were on their feet, thunderously clapping and dancing. The microphones placed among the crowd picked up the audience's excitement and sent it over the airwaves. When Elvis finished "Blue Moon of Kentucky," the crowd wanted more. The *Hayride* had birthed a star!

Presley was offered a one-year contract with the *Hayride*. His parents, Gladys and Vernon Presley, traveled to Shreveport on November 6, 1954, to witness the signing of the contract, since Elvis was underage. He would be paid $18 a performance. Scotty and Bill would each earn $12 a performance. Almost immediately, Elvis traded in his $8 guitar and upgraded to a Martin. The *Louisiana Hayride* served as a booking agency and set up paying performances during the week, which allowed Elvis to quit his day job in Memphis. During the next year, he traveled nearly half a million miles singing his songs. But, during 1955, if it was a Saturday night, Elvis was in Shreveport at the *Louisiana Hayride*.

On the day he signed his one-year contract with the *Hayride*, Elvis made his first and only commercial ad for a product. He sang the Southern Made Doughnuts jingle, "You can get 'em pipin' hot after 4:00 p.m. You can get 'em pipin' hot after 4:00 p.m. You can get 'em pipin' hot. Southern Made Doughnuts hit the spot. You can get 'em piping hot after 4:00 p.m." A year later, Presley signed a $35,000 contract with RCA-Victor records and went on to remarkable fame. On March 3, 1955, he made his first television appearance on the televised *Louisiana Hayride* carried by KSLA-TV, the Shreveport CBS affiliate.

Presley's earlier lackluster *Opry* performance would be his one and only appearance in that venue. But in gratitude to the *Hayride* and Horace Logan, Presley, at the height of his career, agreed to return to the *Hayride* in December 1956. When Presley finished his performance to end the first half of the show, the crowds of young people vacated their seats, stormed the stage, and chased the King into the wings of the concert hall. Meanwhile the live broadcast was still in progress. Logan grabbed the microphone and uttered the famous words, "Please, please, young people . . . Elvis has left the building . . . please take your seats." A most important piece of American broadcasting, the original microphone used by Elvis on his first *Louisiana Hayride* show and the same one used by Logan to utter the famous "Elvis has left the building" phrase, along with the recording of the famous phrase, was auctioned off in California in 2005.

Elvis, the King of Rock and Roll, died on August 16, 1977. Frank Page, the emcee who had introduced a then-unknown Elvis Presley at his debut on the *Louisiana Hayride*, died on January 9, 2013, in Shreveport. Page had retired from KWKH in 2005 after sixty-five years of broadcasting.

The show's name, *The Louisiana Hayride*, was taken from the title of a book by Harnett Thomas Kane on the Louisiana political scandals of 1939–1940. In 1991 the "Muni" was listed on the National Register of Historic Places and was designated a National Historic Landmark in 2008. In 2009, the *Louisiana Hayride* (1948–1960) was inducted into the Louisiana Music Hall of Fame.

RUN, BILLY, RUN!

1959

It was Halloween, October 31, 1959, but few people in Baton Rouge were thinking about trick-or-treating. It was game day and football in the state's capital was king. The Louisiana State University Tigers had enjoyed a perfect record the previous year by scoring a Sugar Bowl victory against South Carolina's Clemson Tigers.

That night's game loomed ominously. It would be a battle between two fierce rivals, the LSU Tigers versus the Old Miss Rebels. It was a home game for the Tigers and expectations were high. Both LSU and Ole Miss came to the contest with no losses for the season. LSU was ranked number one in the nation, Ole Miss was number three, and the highly sought-after national title hung on the outcome of this game.

Saturday dawned gray and the afternoon was soggy. But by the 7:00 p.m. kickoff time, the night was a clear, cool 73 degrees, with 100 percent humidity. The natural grass of the well-manicured LSU football field, used only seven times a year, was wet, and LSU coach Paul Dietzel and Rebels coach Johnny Vaught knew the less-than-perfect conditions would challenge their teams.

A crowd of 67,500 screaming fans crammed the stadium. The war cry, "Go to hell, Ole Miss" was clearly audible in Death Valley, the name given to the LSU football stadium because of the deafening noise levels reached inside.

Both teams had trouble moving the ball on the ground and passes weren't being caught. During the first half, LSU lost three fumbles to Ole Miss. The second fumble had been by left halfback Billy Cannon. It had led to a field goal by Ole Miss, a lead they held until the fourth quarter. LSU's Wendall Harris had attempted a field goal from the Ole Miss thirty-one-yard line, and although he had been successful in his five previous attempts, his wobbler missed the goal posts.

LSU needed a Death Valley miracle. With ten minutes left in the game, that miracle came in the form of an eighty-nine-yard punt return by running back Billy Cannon, with number 20 on his jersey. Cannon was a Baton Rouge hometown boy who wanted to make his family and fans proud. He was a terrific football player and was up for the prestigious Heisman Trophy. Cannon crouched at the ready in the Mississippi end zone. His steely blue eyes watched as Rebel punter Jake Gibbs stepped up to the ball. Gibbs kicked the ball hard and long, angling it knowingly away from Cannon. But a miracle bounce at the sixteen-yard line put the pigskin right into Billy's hands. Cannon scooped up the ball at the eleven-yard line, turned upfield, and began running. At the twenty-yard line, he met his first group of tacklers, but refused to go down, pushing through them with legs pumping. He was hit solidly again. Cannon broke the second tackle, then the third, then the fourth, fifth, sixth, and seventh. Cannon needed only a small crack in the defense to sprint through the gauntlet of Ole Miss tacklers. He raced down the right sideline. By the time he reached the LSU 40-yard line, he had outrun his pursuers. You see the 6'1", 210-pound Cannon was more than a football athlete; he could run the hundred-yard dash in 9.4 seconds, bench-press 435 pounds, and throw a sixteen-pound shot put fifty-four feet. A story goes that Cannon's young wife, sitting (or rather standing) in the stands, became so excited she removed her earrings and tossed them into the crowd. Harris kicked the conversion point. Late in the fourth quarter, Cannon led a goal-line stand and made the game-saving tackle.

The Tigers held on to their lead and with little time left in the game, the crowd started counting down at ten seconds. Then they went crazy! Three students carried Coach Dietzel from the field.

Cannon, a Saturday-night hero, limped toward the sideline. The radio announcer said, "Listen to the cheer for Billy Cannon as he comes off the field. Great All-American." The roar that went up from the crowd was instantaneous and deafening.

Exhausted, Cannon left the field and lay down in the cool, dark tunnel that led to the team's locker rooms. A few minutes later, he made his way to the locker rooms, draped a blue towel around himself, and sprawled out on a training table. Holding an ice pack to his bruised face, he was interviewed by the press and gave credit to his blockers. He said all he was thinking as he headed down the sideline was "run toward your colors and away from theirs." Then Billy changed into street clothes and left the stadium.

"That was the greatest run I ever saw in football," said Coach Dietzel. Cannon won the Heisman Trophy with 519 first-place votes to only 97 for runner-up Richie Lucas of Penn State. Vice president Richard M. Nixon handed him the coveted award.

Billy Cannon's jersey number 20 was retired after the 1959 season. When Cannon's second daughter was born while he was still at LSU, a diaper with the number 20 was hoisted up a flag pole at Tiger Stadium.

Cannon has remained the iconic LSU football player for over fifty years. His "Halloween Run" continues to be played on local radio and television stations. His was the only football number to be retired until 2009. For Death Valley tailgate parties fans paint lavish murals of the Cannon run on the sides of their RVs.

What became of Billy Cannon? After graduating from LSU, Cannon signed with both the AFL and the NFL, an action resulting in a notorious legal battle. He played the professional leagues for eleven years with the Houston Oilers, Oakland Raiders, and Kansas City Chiefs. During his career, he was named All-Pro Halfback and All-Pro Tight end. Billy had sufficient course credits from LSU to be accepted into the University of Tennessee dental school, where he earned a D.D.S. degree. After that, he enrolled in the orthodontia graduate program at Loyola University in Chicago, gaining two additional degrees. Then Billy returned home to practice orthodontia. Youngsters in Louisiana looked eagerly forward to having their teeth fixed by Billy Cannon. In 1983, he was elected to the College Football Hall of Fame.

But trouble loomed ahead for the seemingly invincible Cannon. After a lengthy surveillance, the U.S. Secret Service accused Billy Cannon of being the leader of a counterfeiting scheme, the seventh largest in U.S. history. He immediately confessed, pleading guilty to masterminding the printing of $6 million in counterfeit bills. Several hundred thousand dollars were already in circulation; the rest was buried in Igloo coolers. Cannon, forty-six, was convicted and sent to the minimum-security Federal Correctional Institution in Texarkana, Texas, to serve a five-year term. Two and a half years later, he was out on parole thanks to good behavior. He returned home, where just about everything he'd worked for was gone. Even the College Football Hall of Fame had rescinded its honor.

In 1995, Cannon ironically found work at Angola, the Louisiana State Penitentiary along the Mississippi River. The dental program was in shambles, and Warden Burl Cain hoped Cannon could fix it.

When the program had been put right, Cain put Cannon over the entire medical system, saying, "He got that whole thing organized like a team."

People in Louisiana forgave Billy Cannon, their hero. Today his Heisman trophy is on display in a Baton Rouge sports bar, and he is asked to sign autographs, make personal appearances, and give interviews. Twenty-five years after revoking his membership, and nearly fifty years after his 1959 run, the College Football Hall of Fame reelected him. On November 1, 2003, forty-four years and a day after his famous run, Cannon attended LSU's homecoming game. He stood on the field while his famous run played, larger than life, on the scoreboard. Fans gave him a standing ovation as they cheered wildly. The football players raised their helmets in salute.

When seventy-two-year-old Cannon walks through the front gate at Angola, everyone says hello. He has survived five heart bypasses and cancer, made millions of dollars of counterfeit money, and never explained why. He calls himself and his co-conspirators the dumbest criminals ever. His spare time is spent with his family and a few thoroughbred horses on eleven acres of land outside of St. Francisville, Louisiana.

Today, Death Valley stadium seats 92,400 fans, and it is full every home game. The College Football Association, the *Sporting News*, and *Sport Magazine* say it is the most difficult stadium for a visiting team to play in and ESPN calls Tiger Stadium, "the scariest place to play." Legend has it that in 1988, when LSU fans roared their support for a completed pass that won the game against Auburn, the stamping and cheering registered as an earthquake on a Louisiana seismograph. That game has since been called the "Earthquake Game."

WOODSTOCK FESTIVAL IN RURAL LOUISIANA? NOT!

1971

In June 1971, McCrea, a rural town in Pointe Coupee Parish, on the east bank of the Atchafalaya River, reigned as the site of a rock concert set to rival the legendary Woodstock Music & Art Fair, "An Aquarian Exposition: 3 Days of Peace & Music," held two years earlier. The "Celebration of Life" concert was to be bigger and better. The eight-day festival, produced by the same promoters who had staged the 1970 Atlanta Pop Festival and the Toronto Rock & Roll Revival, was billed as "A Week in the Country Summer Solstice" and advertised as a cross between a rock concert and a renaissance fair. Astrologers, magicians, sitar workshops, and circus acts would be part of the entertainment during the day; the music would play at night when temperatures cooled off.

The official festival poster promised a "large spiritual center" and a "seminar of holy leaders." It listed at least thirty scheduled performers, including the American Rock Opera Company singing selections from *Jesus Christ Superstar*, the Allman Brothers, B. B. King, the

Beach Boys, Bloodrock, Boz Scaggs, Buddy Miles, Canned Heat, Chuck Berry, Country Joe McDonald, It's a Beautiful Day, John B. Sebastian, John Lee Hooker, Leon Russell, Melanie, Ravi Shankar, Seatrain, Sly and the Family Stone, Voices of Harlem, War, Stephen Stills, and Neil Young. There were even rumors that Pink Floyd would make an appearance.

But things went bad from the very beginning. Promoters faced an uphill battle getting a concert venue approved. They first planned the concert in La Place, a town just outside New Orleans, but pressure on the family offering their six-hundred-acre Frenier Beach property led to the agreement being rescinded. Next a site in Mississippi was proposed, but that, too, fell through. Promoter Steve Kapelow was aware that fifty thousand tickets, at $28, had already been sold and that people were showing up in and around New Orleans for the concert set to open on Monday, June 21.

Finally, on June 17, an agreement was reached with a Baton Rouge attorney to lease his soybean plantation for $20,000. Less than twenty-four hours later, Pointe Coupee Parish law enforcement banned the "Celebration of Life," citing lack of adequate sanitary facilities. But by Saturday afternoon, the roads leading to McCrea were jammed. The Louisiana state police set up roadblocks and told festivalgoers the concert was cancelled. Thousands of young people, many of whom had traveled long distances, could not be persuaded to leave. They set up camps along the road and waited. At a press conference the local officials of Pointe Coupee Parish asked the governor and the National Guard for assistance in closing down the concert. Concert promoters appealed the decision to the Fifth U.S. Circuit Court of Appeals in New Orleans, which ruled in their favor. The concert was back on and ticket holders would be allowed entry to the site beginning Sunday morning, June 20.

By the start of the concert on Monday, thousands of young people had flooded into the area along the levee. Some from as far away as New York and Ohio had been camping out for days. Some had tickets, many did not. They came by car and on foot. Many hitchhiked. Vans decorated with flower decals and filled with "flower children" loped down the country roads, dirt billowing in their wakes. Traffic jams were common. Cars were directed to park in muddy fields where, while waiting for entry, shirtless young people sprawled on the hoods of their cars, and some found places to nap in the open trunks of their automobiles. Big speakers playing music from tops of vans added to the festive air.

Meanwhile, construction crews worked feverishly to complete the thirty-foot stage and sound system so that the concert, already three days late, could begin on Thursday evening. Their work was hampered by the unstable ground. The top soil layer was weakly supported by wet mud fed by the underground tributaries of the Atchafalaya River. During a bad afternoon thunderstorm, the stage scaffolding gave way and collapsed.

Law enforcement was still trying to close down the concert. Louisiana governor John McKeithen had vowed to personally evict the "long-haired, dope-group anarchists." But by the time the state police got to McCrea and attempted to blockade the entrance, it was too late. Thousands had already staked out plots of grass on which to erect tents or lay their blankets. Pointe Coupee deputies on horses were sent in to patrol the area. But it became impossible to corral all the people through the ticket gates. Many took advantage of the chaos to sneak in free of charge.

Because of the postponed performances, thousands of young people amused themselves by cooling off, nude, in the muddy waters of the Atchafalaya. They made human mud pies, lathering on the Atchafalaya mud that when it dried turned a bluish color. Naked blue "mud people" strolled the venue. Groups divided into "water" people and "mud" people. During "wars," water people tried to rinse the mud off of mud people and mud people countered with smearing water people with mud. Nude sunbathing was popular, too, as was lounging on blankets while passing around joints. Locals were outraged by the crowd swell of seventy thousand youths and their "hippie" behavior.

Despite the blistering heat, oppressive humidity, and three days of delays, hopes for a great "Celebration of Life" were still high. The festival finally got underway on Thursday night at 6:00 p.m. with a colorful fireworks display. Then the stage lights illuminated guru Yogi Bhajan, who took the stage chanting, "God bless you. Let us meditate for one minute for peace and brotherhood." The first day's lineup included John Sebastian, a veteran Woodstock performer who opened the concert, followed by Country Joe McDonald, Brownsville Station, Eric Bourdon & War, Bloodrock, and Jimmy Witherspoon. By 3:00 a.m. Chuck Berry in his wild, flowered pants outfit was on stage belting out his latest number-one hit, "My Ding-A-Ling."

The next two days brought new problems. Ticket holders had been promised food in the price of their tickets. That amounted to a truck rolling by once a day tossing out watermelons. Water trucks provided limited rations as well. A tractor pulling a flatbed trailer collected the endless piles of discarded rotting watermelon rinds, empty wine bottles, and abandoned clothing. Festival promoters had hired the Galloping Goose, Vikings, and Wheelers, motorcycle clubs from New Orleans, to provide security. They, in fact, weren't doing the job, but until the legalities were cleared up, law enforcement officers left the policing of the campsites and river area to the bikers. But things soon got out of hand. Many festivalgoers had been on-site for four or five days, and food, water, and money were becoming critically scarce. The few vendors had run out of most items by Thursday evening, and those that hadn't had been overrun by hungry hippies who "liberated" the remaining inventory. By Friday, both promoters and attendees complained the weapon-brandishing motorcyclists were stealing food and beating up festival participants. They urged the Pointe Coupee Parish sheriff to step in. As drugs had become more prevalent, the bikers had also taken to robbing dealers of their stash and their profits. Homemade signs marked the intersection of Cocaine Row and Smack Streets, where large sums of money changed hands. On Friday afternoon, local and state police moved in in storm-trooper fashion, stripped the bikers of weapons, and evicted the motorcycle club members. One hundred and fifty National Guardsmen stood on alert in nearby New Roads waiting to assist. The police who took control had guns, too, and arrested many of the youths; state undercover narcotics agents made more than one hundred busts. On Friday, Ted Nugent took the stage. He was unhappy that much of the crowd was sleeping through his performance. The Amboy Dukes; Stoneground; the promised "surprise band" from San Francisco, Bloodrock; and a few other bands played for the crowd.

The summer sun was brutal and shade was nonexistent. The *New York Times* described the festival site as a "sun-scorched pasture" that resembled a labor camp out of the Dust Bowl era. The 96- to 109-degree days were blistering hot, as were the nights, but there were added inconveniences. Many attendees reported a deafening buzz of insects through the swampy midsummer nights. Others spoke of armadillos circling their campfires. Some heavy thunderstorms did roll through the area in the afternoon, with rain that came down so hard, the pelting actually hurt. The rain didn't cool things off, and when the ferocious sun came back out, the air became a steam bath.

During the day on Saturday, The Rolling Stones' new album *Sticky Fingers* and The Beatles' *Sgt. Pepper's Lonely Hearts Club Band* rang out over and over on a speaker system. The kids continued to frolic in the Atchafalaya, ignoring warnings about water moccasins. A circus act featuring Molly Cova's high-wire act was set up near the stage. That evening again saw an abbreviated roster of performers due to the return of the rains that had made such a muddy mess of things earlier in the week. Melanie opened the evening, singing like an angel for a full solo set that included "Brand New Key" and "Lay Down (Candles in the Rain)." An up-and-coming southern band with a new record, Black Oak Arkansas, also performed. Near sunrise, It's a Beautiful Day, one of the most remembered acts of the concert, pleased the crowd with their soulful flute music of "White Bird." To the surprise of those still awake, skydivers floated to the ground against the pink swirls of early dawn.

On Sunday, the crowd was treated to the music of Stephen Stills and Neil Young, who had flown down to New Orleans and arrived by helicopter to salvage the concert. But as they finished their set, the plug was pulled. The Internal Revenue Service placed a $700,000 tax lien against the festival, and the "Celebration of Life" was officially over. At the end of four days, three people were dead. The swift river currents of the Atchafalaya River claimed two of the youths, and another died from a drug overdose. A *Time Magazine* article, "Mud, Sweat & Tears," on July 12, 1971, called the "Celebration of Life" a nightmare that marked the end of the "beatific American experience" begun at Woodstock.

Records of the festival are sketchy at best, relying mostly on the memories of young people, high on life and/or marijuana. Although cameras were prohibited, a few people managed to sneak cameras past the sheriff's deputies. A documentary film, *McCrea 1971*, aired in 2014 on Louisiana cable channels. It featured digitalized 16 mm and 35 mm film clips; interviews with musicians, including the late Stephen Stills Band guitarist, Stephen Fromholz; and interviews with attendees of the festival. The documentary has been chosen for several film festivals and screenings in the state. Most personal accounts of the event reflect that the young people of 1971 went to McCrea, Louisiana, for the music, and took away an unforgettable experience.

THE CASE OF THE DISAPPEARING
FRESHWATER LAKE

1980

Lake Peigneur was a freshwater lake in southern Louisiana Cajun country near New Iberia. It lazily emptied into Vermillion Bay via the Delcambre Canal and then made its way to the Gulf of Mexico. The thirteen-hundred-acre shallow lake was an unremarkable but popular place for fishermen and naturalists. Besides its warm temperatures and magnificent oak trees, the area was also home to a huge salt dome and petroleum resources below the ground.

Here's the story of how that quiet, idyllic lake changed significantly and permanently on a Thursday morning, November 20, 1980.

The hundred-year-old Diamond Crystal Salt Company had been operating its Jefferson Island salt mine under Lake Peigneur since the early 1900s. Scores of shafts extended several thousand feet into the salt dome. At the same time Texaco, operating a rig owned by the Wilson Brothers Corporation, was drilling a test hole, Well No. 20, through the bottom of the lake.

Everything was going smoothly until about 4:30 a.m., when the drilling equipment seized up at 1,228 feet below the lake. The five-man crew tried to free the drilling assembly, but neither jarring nor "working" the pipe was successful. The crew heard a series of loud pops, and by the time the seven-man shift showed up two hours later, the rig had begun to list. Fearing a collapse was imminent, the men radioed Texaco's office in New Iberia and loosened the attached barges, and then both crews abandoned the $5 million rig and headed for shore some two hundred yards away.

Texaco was aware of the salt mine and had reportedly planned carefully to avoid it, but a miscalculation placed the drilling rig directly above one of the upper salt mine shafts. The search for oil had resulted in a fourteen-inch drill bit puncturing the roof of the third level of the adjacent Diamond salt mine. The water in the lake began to pour into the cavernous mine shafts below.

On shore, the crew watched in amazement as the huge platform and 140-foot derrick overturned and then surprisingly disappeared into lake water that was less than ten feet deep. Soon the water around where the rig had disappeared began to swirl. It turned slowly at first, but steadily accelerated until a fast-moving whirlpool a quarter of a mile in diameter was directly over the drilling site.

As the whirlpool grew, an electrician working in the salt mines below heard a strange, loud noise. He discovered fuel drums banging against each other as they were carried along the mine shaft by a stream of muddy water. He heard water gurgling overhead and immediately sounded the evacuation alarm. As emergency lights flashed, the paging system notified the miners to get out. The nine workers on the thirteen-hundred-foot level hopped onto the mine's small steel elevator cage and were lifted to safety. The other forty-one miners were at the fifteen-hundred-foot fourth level below the surface. They ran for their lives to the upper, thirteen-hundred-foot level, but the corridors were by this time blocked by waist-deep water. They used carts and diesel-powered vehicles to drive to the one-thousand-foot level, where they could access an elevator. The elevator could hold only eight or nine men at a time and it seemed to take forever for all of the miners to escape the collapsing salt dome.

Throughout the morning, the original fourteen-inch hole expanded as water, land, soil, and debris were sucked in by the huge whirlpool and rushed into the enormous empty underground spaces created by years of salt removal. Residents and rig employees watched in horror as a parking lot, house trailers, tractors, and tons of mud vanished into the whirlpool. There was nothing anyone could do but watch. Louisiana State Police captain, Louis Ackal, stood with others as swirls of mud sucked giant oak trees "like a hand pulling them into the mud." A natural gas fire was reported near where the oil rig had been drilling.

The twelve-mile Delcambre Canal, which usually carried water away from the freshwater lake through Vermilion Bay to the salty Gulf of Mexico, reversed itself and became a temporary inflow waterway, carrying tons of salt water into the area. Another oil rig and eleven barges on the canal joined the swirling vortex on the lake's surface. A tugboat struggling at full throttle could not avoid the pull of the flow dragging it down the canal and into the Lake Peigneur sinkhole. Crew members leapt off the tug and swam safely toward the canal bank. The backflow from the canal eventually fell 164 feet into the newly created crater, filling the lake and salt mines with salt water and temporarily creating the tallest waterfall ever in Louisiana. As the water flooded into the mines, the pillars of salt, strategically left to support the eighty-foot-high ceilings of tunnels as wide as four-lane highways, were dissolved by the lake water. The pillars collapsed. Because the air in the mine could not get out faster than the water was coming in, the compressed air created geysers that shot up four hundred feet, spraying water and accumulated debris into the air.

After two days the lake stabilized. An estimated 3.5 billion gallons of salt water had been sucked in from the Gulf of Mexico, and seventy acres of land had disappeared into the sinkhole. Once the water pressure equalized, nine of the eleven sunken barges popped out of the whirlpool like corks and emerged on the lake's surface. The drilling rigs and tug were never seen again.

But the lake had changed. The once freshwater ten-foot-deep lake was now a saltwater lake with a depth of thirteen hundred feet, and the ecosystem has been irrevocably altered by the increased salt content in the water.

Miraculously, there was no loss of life. All salt mine employees escaped, rig workers fled the platform before it was sucked down, and a local fisherman and his nephew on the lake at the time were able to walk away from the fourteen-foot aluminum boat when it got stuck in the mud as the water rushed out of the lake. The Delcambre Canal was naturally dredged, and it is two to four feet deeper.

It was difficult for researchers to determine exactly what happened; the evidence had been destroyed or washed away. The Mine Safety and Health Administration was not able to apportion blame. Confusion over whether Texaco was drilling in the wrong place or whether the mine's maps were inaccurate could not be ascertained. Nonetheless, Texaco and the Wilson Brothers Corporation paid out-of-court settlements of $32 million to Diamond Crystal for damages to its mine and $12.8 million to nearby Live Oak Gardens, a wholesale nursery. The mine was closed in December 1986.

Since 1994, the vacated salt dome at Lake Peigneur has been used as storage area for pressurized natural gas. Citizens and local officials have pleaded with the governor to stop an expected expansion of the storage operation in the fragile area, where intermittent bubbles have recently been observed escaping from the salt dome, but to no avail.

THOUSANDS SEEK
THE VIRGIN MARY

1989

In 1987, Alfredo Raimondo, a devote Catholic and Tunisian immigrant, was leading an ordinary life. He was married with children and working as a pipe fitter in a New Orleans shipyard. One day he was inspired to take a trip to Medjugorje, Yugoslavia, a popular pilgrimage site where the Blessed Virgin Mary had reportedly appeared to six youths. He followed the footsteps of thousands of Catholic pilgrims, climbed the miraculous mountaintop, and left inspired.

He returned to his simple life, but his world would never be the same again. Alfredo was visited by the Virgin Mary where he lived in Chalmette, an area just outside New Orleans. She said she was pleased that so many people in the area had visited her at Medjugorje and asked for a special mass to be said for St. Joseph, her husband. She promised to perform miracles if this were to happen.

Alfredo was a changed man after this vision. He quit his job as a menial laborer, left his wife temporarily behind, and took off for Tickfaw, a small village about fifty miles north of New Orleans, where he had a one-room trailer and seven acres of empty land. Alfredo dedicated himself to his religious calling and spent the next year in meditation and prayer.

Alfredo wanted to make sure the St. Joseph celebration, requested by Our Lady, happened. He began to talk of her promise to perform miracles and, as word circulated into the rural community, volunteers offered to help. Alfredo's Tickfaw property, located between the Antioch Baptist Church and the Sisters of St. Benedict Monastery, seemed the most appropriate spot for the mass. Sunday, March 12, 1989, a week before the official designation of St. Joseph's Feast Day held annually on March 19, was set for the big day. The Virgin Mary who made the request became known as Our Lady of Tickfaw.

Alfredo's story received national media attention. Police Capt. Ted Panning told a newspaper reporter, "We have had calls from all over. I understand there will be charter buses from all over the world." The small southeastern Louisiana town of just five hundred people was about to be inundated with thousands of pilgrims seeking a religious experience. Fifty law enforcement officers from neighboring towns had been called in to help with crowd control.

In preparation for the event, Alfredo had set up a large wooden cross and a statue of the Sacred Heart of Jesus at what would serve as the center of the gathering. Here an open-air mass was scheduled to be said. Devout Roman Catholics and some not so devout, but nevertheless inspired by Alfredo's vision and the Virgin Mary's request, showed up by the thousands. Travelers said they weren't sure a miracle would happen, but they knew Our Lady wanted them to be here, and so they came. Others hoped desperately for spiritual and physical healing.

Families arrived with lawn chairs and coolers. Picnic lunches were set out in the eighty-degree weather. Women with floral crosses at their sides knelt in the backwoods dirt to pray. Other believers knelt before a St. Joseph's Altar heaped high with food and flowers before a picture of the Last Supper. Hail Mary recitations could be heard over a loudspeaker. Alfredo began wandering among the great number of visitors, many of whom reached out to touch the man who had been chosen by the Virgin Mary. Alfredo was content and happy with the turnout of the faithful.

Confessions were heard by three priests who attended the celebration. A New Orleans priest heard confessions for five hours, reporting, "Some people said it had been 10, 20, 30 years since they had been to confession. Some people had tears running down their faces."

Praying continued after the mass. People described strange rays of light coming from the sun. Children said they saw visions of the Blessed Mother. Those fortunate enough to be visited by Our Lady of Tickfaw said her message was, "Pray for peace, pray from the heart." Rosaries and Catholic medals dangling from the hands of believers were seen to change from silver to gold tone; others reported the strong scent of Mary's roses, though no rosebushes were on or near the property. Testimonials of the pilgrims expressed faith and hope, saying that they had experienced what they had come for. "I believe that I saw her, Jesus, Joseph and the angels and the saints," said a young woman from Covington. Another woman from Luling pointed to a fuzzy snapshot and said, "See, here's the Blessed Mother."

Later in the day, a healing service was held and healings were reported. A miracle seeker from nearby Hammond said she had seen the gates of heaven and expressed hope that her glaucoma and her uncle's cancer would be cured.

After dark, a candlelight procession ended the day of prayer. The county sheriff's deputy remarked that the event was the first time in twelve years of directing traffic that nobody had complained to him and noted, "This is the nicest, most well-behaved group of people." Some reports say as many as eight to ten thousand people showed up to honor Our Lady of Tickfaw.

The believers did not stop coming. A prayer group formed to meet every day to pray the rosary. Additions were made to the site. A three-tier fountain was built at the exact spot where a spring had been revealed to a believer in a vision. The clear sparkling water, from which the faithful can fill containers to take home, was blessed by a priest on October 7, 1990. A life-size carving of the crucified Christ was erected just behind a small shrine, and a Medjugorje statue of Our Lady of Peace was placed near the newly built sanctuary of the Holy Spirit. Other statues of the Virgin dedicated to Our Lady of Forgiveness and Our Lady of Consolation have been set amid the religious landscape.

During the year, Alfredo had received another vision from Mary, who asked him to bake bread to feed the people who visited her "sacred ground." An oven was constructed, and the man building the oven reported seeing Mary overlooking his work. Other believers spoke of visions of Mary standing contentedly behind the oven. Bread was baked on Sunday mornings and offered free to all visitors. The faithful have reported visions, conversions, and healings. The Bishop of Baton Rouge investigated the events and declared that the spiritual fruits resulting from the alleged apparitions were numerous. However he chose not to pronounce a canonical judgment on the origin of the apparitions.

Tickfaw became known as the Medjugorje of Tangipahoa Parish, and for nearly twenty years an endless stream of cars and buses lined up along the road to the shrine, and even walkers poured into the area. Every year on the Feast of St. Joseph, mass is held and a traditional St. Joseph's Altar, laden with food, is constructed. Raimondo has since died, and his family is trying to keep up the seven-acre shrine and more than a hundred religious statues, which include the Virgin Mary in her various roles, such as Our Lady of Guadalupe, Our Lady of Mt. Carmel, and Our Lady of Fatima. The saints are there, too: St. Anne, St. Francis of Assisi, and St. Joseph. The holy water fountain, said to wash away rashes, goiters, and even more serious ailments, is now dry.

MARDI GRAS SHIPWRECK CELEBRATES HISTORY UNDERWATER

2007

In the 1800s, New Orleans was a bustling port and trading center. It was an important shipping point for products bound for both foreign and domestic ports. Major exports through the port city were cotton, sugar, coffee, and tobacco, as well as flour, butter, cattle, knives, and ammunition. New Orleans was a vital port for trade to South and Central America, especially to the islands, which depended on U.S. flour, beans, beef, whiskey, and chewing tobacco. Cuban exports welcomed in the United States included coffee, tortoise shell, molasses, mahogany, paper, and dry goods. Schooners carrying people and products to and from various countries were plentiful, but the Gulf of Mexico was a dangerous place. French privateers engaged in illicit trade in the Caribbean, attacking both U.S. and English ships. Cunning pirates patrolled the seas, looking to illegally seize booty from whichever ships came their way. Colonial conflicts were rampant, and the United States was fighting to protect its waters. The 1803 Haitian revolt against slaveholders increased the demand for illegal slaves. Spanish tariffs were still in place as part of the France–Spain alliance for control of New Orleans and the Mississippi River. British naval activity was considered enemy action to the French in the Caribbean as well as to the infamous Louisiana Barataria Bay buccaneers, Jean Lafitte and his band of smugglers. The United States declared war on Great Britain in 1812, revolution in Texas was beginning, and as Spain was growing weaker and lost colonies in the area, the port of New Orleans and her shipbuilding industry became vital to the sea battles ahead. All in all, the Gulf of Mexico was a pretty hazardous waterway.

Many of the large seafaring vessels were built in the shipyards of New Orleans using southern yellow pine native to Louisiana. The yellow pine was favored as a building material for frames and spars because it was strong and sturdy, yet easy to work with. The smaller, two-masted schooners with lightweight hulls for better navigating the shallow harbors were also constructed here. Many merchants preferred the smaller vessel to avoid predators. Many of those doing the preying also liked the smaller, more maneuverable ships to avoid detection. Gunrunning was also a profitable and common practice among the nefarious types lurking in the Gulf of Mexico.

It was in this milieu that, just after the War of 1812 broke out, a New Orleans hotel owner secured a letter of mark for the schooner the *Rapid* to cruise against the enemies of the United States. The mission of the *Rapid* was to attack British vessels. This directive was collaborated by a November 20, 1813, entry in the log of a British warship, the HMS *Herald*. The *Herald* claims to have set upon a chase of the *Rapid* off the coast of Louisiana when a squall arose. The *Rapid* sunk in the rain, wind, and turbulence. The *Herald* records rescuing the master and crew of the ship, who were treated as prisoners of war.

Fast-forward two hundred years later. . . . In 2002, an inspection crew recorded a blip on the floor of the Gulf of Mexico, thirty-five miles off the Louisiana coast, during a routine oilfield survey for a new deep natural gas pipeline. No remains of a ship had been previously recorded in the area. Because the pressure at four thousand feet below the ocean would crush a human being, a remotely operated vehicle (ROV) was requisitioned and sent down into the deep warm gulf waters. The robot beamed back a snapshot of early 1800 history: the remains of a two-hundred-year-old sailing vessel. A team of sixty scientists and technicians led by Texas A&M took charge of the recovery operation, with funding from the Okeanos Gas Gathering Co. and the U.S. Minerals Management Service. Nautilus Productions was selected to create a documentary. Every task performed on the seabed, including detailed mapping of the artifacts and 3D imaging of the parts of the ship and its position, was documented on video with as much resolution as possible provided by high-resolution digital still cameras with high-intensity lights.

Five years later, on May 21, 2007, the historic site was ready for excavation. The Mardi Gras Shipwreck project, named because it was located next to the Mardi Gras pipeline, was the first project in deep water to use archeological principles and was, at that time, the deepest archaeological scientific endeavor ever attempted. In addition to high-resolution cameras, lighting systems, and imaging and positioning sonar equipment, the project operated two ROV systems that were completely fiber-optic and supported by eight cameras. The 256-foot-long *Toisa Vigilant*, an ROV support vessel, complete with a helipad and giant cranes, was the scientists' work platform, living quarters, and laboratory during the project. The *Toisa Vigilant* was docked at Port Fourchon, Louisiana's southernmost port. Large artifact retrieval tools (LARTs) recovered large artifacts using two scooping arms that could be closed at a controlled rate by means of hydraulic rams. Small artifacts were collected by suction pickers and scoops. One of the biggest challenges for excavators was that the site had very little current, so when the fine silt was disturbed during excavation, it was not carried off. Loss of visibility meant recovery mapping, and photography was impaired, often for hours.

All recovered artifacts were transported to College Station, Texas, to be conserved and labeled. After that process, they will become the property of the Division of Archaeology of the Louisiana Department of Culture, Recreation and Tourism.

The center of the Mardi Gras Shipwreck Project was a medium-sized schooner, thought to have sailed the gulf waters sometime between 1808 and 1820. The Minerals Management Service (MMS) and archaeological researchers speculatively identified the vessel as the U.S. privateer ship, the *Rapid*. The ship's hull of yellow pine wood was found resting on and partly embedded in a nearly level ocean bottom made up of silty clay. The hull above the sediment had been both worn away by natural tidal action and destroyed by boring mollusks. On the eighth day of excavation, a large basket of artifacts broke the surface of the water, and approximately six hundred artifacts were eventually recovered from it.

What was found? Archeologists uncovered an iron anchor, a cast-iron stove, and two pewter spoons that, although bent and scratched, look almost new. Navigational instruments, including a preserved captain's telescope with a brass eyepiece with the name and place of its manufacture found by X-ray, part of an octant, and the remains of two compasses, were also discovered. Fourteen complete or nearly complete glass bottles were found, as well as several glass fragments. Some of the glassware was typical of French wineglasses of the time period, ranging in color from deep green to dark brown. Dark green and light blue British bottles were also in evidence. Other artifacts included tableware, a couple of sets of ceramic dishes, and a stoneware jug. Two personal items were unearthed: a leather shoe heel and a toothbrush head and handle. Researchers found eight coffee beans and a coffee grinder. The *Rapid*, if indeed it is, was carrying a quantity of arms and ammunition, much of which still rests on the seafloor. This arms cache included a six-pounder cannon that, according to markings, was made at the Clyde Iron Works in Scotland in 1797; a box of seventeen mixed weapons, such as muskets; seven pistols; over 2,600 lead shot; sixty gunflints; and edged weapons such as sabers or cutlasses.

The shipwreck and her artifacts will yield time capsule information on the history of the Gulf of Mexico, the beginning years of the United States, details of military missions and weapons, and valuable insight into the everyday lives of the men who sailed the waters beyond Louisiana. The restored artifacts are housed at Texas A&M University's Conservation Research Laboratory, and some are on display at the Louisiana State Museum in New Orleans. The documentary, *Mystery Mardi Gras Shipwreck*, won a 2009 bronze Telly Award.

MORE THAN JUST AN OILY MESS

2010

The Gulf of Mexico, formed nearly three hundred million years ago, has always been a vital part of Louisiana's own history. The Mississippi River, which drains the state's bayous, canals, and smaller waterways, flows through a rich delta region and empties into its saltwater ocean basin. The Gulf of Mexico played a pivotal role when brothers Pierre Le Moyne d'Iberville colonized Louisiana and Jean Baptiste Le Moyne de Bienville founded New Orleans in 1718. It witnessed a lucrative pirate smuggling trade and the defense of New Orleans against the British in the 1800s. The last two hundred years were less turbulent, but the Gulf of Mexico has seen its share of earthquakes, hurricanes, and oil rig disasters. Its stretches of sandy beaches, its numerous barrier islands, and the warm Gulf Stream current make the Gulf Coast a favorite beach lover's paradise. The Gulf of Mexico washing Louisiana's coast is home to 8,332 species of fish, birds, mollusks, crustaceans, sea turtles, and marine mammals. But man could not let this wonder of nature alone, for there is oil beneath its waters.

History would mark April 20, 2010, as the date of the largest oil spill and biggest man-made disaster ever to impact the state. It would bring ruin to marine and marsh animals, aquatic plants, sea life, ecosystems, related commercial industries, and the livelihoods of the hunters, fishermen, and shrimpers of Louisiana vitally dependent on the health of the gulf and the areas sustained by it.

The Deepwater Horizon platform, a nine-year-old semi-submersible oil-drilling rig, was operated by British Petroleum (BP) in the Macondo Prospect, located in the Mississippi Canyon just forty miles off the coast of Louisiana. The rig, built by a South Korean company and owned by Transocean, was chartered to BP and could operate in depths of up to ten thousand feet of water. When the disaster happened, the rig was drilling an exploratory well 35,050 feet deep in 5,100 feet of water. On that fateful Tuesday spring evening, at approximately 9:45 p.m. local time, pressurized methane gas expanded into the drilling riser and then filled the drilling rig, where it ignited. The oil rig exploded and engulfed the platform; 126 men were aboard the drilling rig. Most of the crew was rescued by lifeboats and helicopters. The U.S. Coast Guard searched relentlessly for three days for eleven missing men, but to no avail—the explosion had claimed their lives.

After the explosion, the seafloor began to spew out oil; the rig sank a day and a half later. On April 24, BP announced its estimate that one thousand barrels of oil a day were emptying into the gulf; on April 29, the U.S. government estimated five thousand barrels of oil a day were leaking into the gulf from the wellhead; and, by May 27, U.S. Geological Survey revised its figures to report that twelve to nineteen thousand barrels of oil a day were being discharged into the Gulf of Mexico.

By early June, oil had washed up on 125 miles of the Louisiana coastline, and by July oily tar balls had reached Grand Isle,

Louisiana's only inhabited barrier island. Miles of beaches and wildlife were affected by the intruding substance. Also in July, evidence of the oil spill showed up on the shores of Lake Pontchartrain, an inland, brackish estuary of the Gulf of Mexico, and one of the largest wetlands in the world. This popular lake, bordering New Orleans, is located in six Louisiana parishes and covers an area of 630 square miles.

The effects on coastal wetlands, marine life, and estuaries that fed the entire delta area were devastating. Clean-up actions were put into motion immediately and included floating booms, skimmer ships, chemical dispersants, and controlled burns. Residents of the state along the coast turned to prayer, paper towels to wipe the oil off marsh grasslands, and homemade barriers to arrest the flow of the oily residue into their lives.

The oil continued to spill into the gulf, day after day, week after week, month after month. Finally, after eighty-eight days, on July 15, 2010, BP announced the leak was sealed off; and, on September 19, the BP oil well was officially declared "dead" by the federal government. The total discharge of oil into the Gulf of Mexico was estimated at 4.9 million barrels. Satellite images show that the spill spread to sixty-eight thousand square miles of the gulf, an area roughly the size of Oklahoma.

The spill endangered not only the fourteen species of wildlife under federal protection, which included sea turtles, alligators, and bottlenose dolphins, but also an additional thirty-nine species of birds, mammals, fish, crustaceans, and other wildlife. The first oily seabird found offshore in Louisiana was a long-beaked, yellow-crowned northern gannet. Wildlife rescue teams from the Delaware-based Tri-State Bird Rescue and Research set up in historic Fort Jackson, about seventy miles southeast of New Orleans, to help with animal rescue. The young bird was washed clean from the BP oil with dish detergent and scrubbed with a toothbrush. It was also given medicine for an upset stomach. Louisiana brown pelicans, the state bird recently taken off the endangered species list, were threatened anew as they struggled in the oily mess. Other animals still at risk include the endangered Kemp's Ridley sea turtle, which has been on the Louisiana critically endangered species list since 1989; whale sharks, the biggest fish in the ocean, living up to seventy years; dolphins; sperm whales; and bluefin tuna and their hatching eggs. Louisiana authorities closed down oyster beds, shrimping grounds, and all commercial and recreational fishing east of the Mississippi River. Damage to the gulf floor especially hurt the Louisiana pancake batfish, an unusual-looking fish that made the Arizona State University International Institute for Species Exploration's top-ten list of newly discovered species. The habitat range of the flat, two-inch-long bottom dweller, so named because it is flat like a pancake and walks like a bat, was entirely contained within the area affected by the oil spill. Other residual effects include the death of a coral community and of marine life in a radius thirty to fifty miles around the well.

The U.S. government faulted BP, Deepwater Horizon operator Transocean, and contractor Halliburton, leading to civil and criminal prosecutions and over 130 private lawsuits. In 2012, BP settled the federal case by pleading guilty to eleven counts of manslaughter and agreeing to pay a record-breaking $4.525 billion in fines and payouts. Today environmental and health consequences continue to be studied and investigated. Some reports indicate the well site may still be leaking. BP claims it has spent $6 million a day on clean-up efforts; the cost to the Louisiana fishing and shrimping industries, tourism, and wildlife cannot be measured. The U.S. Environmental Protection Agency (EPA) created air quality monitoring stations along Louisiana's Plaquemines Parish on the coast. The agency also monitors the presence of several chemicals in the environment, such

as xylene, benzene, and toluene. It has established a website (www
.epa.gov/bpspill/) to provide information about the spill's effect on
environmental and health concerns. Another site, www.restorethegulf
.gov, keeps the public informed of ongoing issues.

In 2012, oil sheens could still be found along Louisiana coastline
and tar balls continued to wash up along the sandy coast. In 2013,
scientists at the Gulf of Mexico Oil Spill and Ecosystem Science
Conference said that as much as one-third of the oil may have mixed
with deep ocean sediments, where it continues to damage ecosystems
and commercial fisheries. In the first dolphin birthing season after the
spill, dead baby dolphins washed up at ten times the normal number,
most with oil residue on their bodies. Other dolphins were found to
be underweight, anemic, and suffering from lung and liver disease.
Evidence of oil and dispersant was found in the zooplankton and
under the shells of blue crab larvae. Migratory birds carried chemicals
related to the oil spill as far as Minnesota, and a sample test of pelican
eggs revealed high levels of petroleum compounds. Fish with sores
and lesions were first noted by fishermen, and chemicals from the
oil and cleanup are believed to have caused numbers of mutated fish,
including shrimp lacking eyes and eye sockets.

The environmental impacts continue, and research is ongoing. In
2013, researchers found that oil on the bottom of the seafloor does
not appear to be degrading, creating an underwater "dirty blizzard" of
oily particles. The result could have long-term effects on both human
and marine life as oil and related chemicals can remain in the food
chain for generations.

STILL MAKING THE *GUINNESS* BOOK OF WORLD RECORDS

2011

In the early 1800s, wealthy developer Bernard de Marigny owned a third of the city of New Orleans, including the fashionable area downriver from the French Quarter known as Marigny. But he wanted to expand his holdings, and so he purchased land from the Bonnabel and Davis families on the north side of Lake Pontchartrain, a 630-square-mile, brackish lake abutting New Orleans. The lake, named after Count de Pontchartrain, minister to King Louis XIV of France, for whom Louisiana is named, is home to a variety of fish, ducks, and the beloved brown pelican. Age-old trees draped with Spanish moss line its banks. Marigny's holdings became Fontainebleau Plantation, and included a sugar mill and brick factory. Marigny eventually bought more land and in 1834 developed the village of Mandeville. Unique to Marigny's vision for Mandeville was the founding provision that the land fronting Lake Pontchartrain be held for all residents as public land, never built on and never fenced. As the town grew, restaurants, hotels, and a gambling casino drew residents and visitors to Mandeville. Marigny provided a ferry service to bring people from New Orleans, forty miles on the other side of the lake, to the popular resort area. The two-and-a-half-hour steamboat excursion ran from the Milneburg dock north of New Orleans to the beachside area in Mandeville. By 1850 fourteen sawmills and fifteen brickyards had been built, and over ninety steamboats were navigating the waterways to supply the continued growth of the area. Marigny's ferry services continued into the twentieth century.

In the 1920s, a proposal was made suggesting the creation of a series of artificial islands on the lake that could be linked to each other by bridges. This road system would ultimately link New Orleans with Mandeville. Financing the plan rested on the idea of selling homesites on the islands. The project failed to garner enough interest.

In 1948, a new plan was proposed for a concrete bridge to cross the middle of the lake. By 1954, the Louisiana Bridge Company was making plans for construction of this bridge using prefabricated bridge sections that would be transported by barge to the assembly site. Construction began on May 23, 1955, with the sinking of the first pilings into the lake. Revolutionary construction techniques were utilized, including using over nine thousand pre-stressed concrete pilings of fifty-four-inch-diameter steel-reinforced posts and steam-curing processes.

The $30 million bridge was a wonder! It spanned 23.83 miles over the center of Lake Pontchartrain, finally connecting Metairie, a suburb of New Orleans, to Mandeville on the north shore. The bridge was called the Lake Pontchartain Causeway and, remarkably, it opened four months ahead of schedule on August 30, 1956. This modern marvel of human ingenuity and engineering was entered into the *Guinness Book of World Records* as the longest bridge over water in the world. Those traveling the bridge are struck by the vista, eight miles out, which includes only water and the thin horizon. No land is visible for the next eight miles.

The Causeway was a huge convenience for commuters and travelers, reducing travel time by fifty minutes as they navigated the insipid waterways endemic to southern Louisiana. By 1967 there was a clamor for more lanes. Instead of simply adding more lanes to the existing bridge and in the interest of vehicular safety, a parallel bridge was planned; each span, eighty-four feet apart, would have one-way traffic. The $26 million northbound span, opened on May 10, 1969, was a little longer than the southbound lane. Its 23.87-mile span was added to the record book.

But 2011 brought an end to the fifty-five-year-old record held by the Lake Pontchartrain Causeway. Halfway around the world, the 26.4-mile Jiaozhou Bay Bridge was nearing its $2.3 billion completion in China. The Causeway would lose its long-standing record because of a two-and-a-half-mile deficit! The people of Louisiana were upset, for there was little they could do. But the Causeway was still first in the hearts of the citizenry who needed to cross the lake each day. During Hurricane Katrina, the Causeway sustained only minimal damage on one of its seven turnaround sections, but the bridge was closed for about a month for repair and inspection. When it reopened, as a concession to hurricane victims, tolls were eliminated for the next month. A radio station and 102 call boxes are part of the bridge's safety infrastructure. Variable message signs (VMSs) alert motorists to any hazards along the bridge span. They can announce an accident, slow traffic, or construction delays. In response to and since the 9/11 terrorist attacks, the VMS displayed patriotic messages such as "God Bless America." The use of VMS road message signs to communicate non-road-related messages is unique to the Causeway.

But Louisianans were not ready to accept defeat so easily. Many simply refused to acknowledge the bridge in China. Some said that the bridge didn't qualify because part of the Chinese bridge actually doubled back to the main span from a landmass and so that distance could be counted only once. Many said it was enough for them that the Causeway was the longest in the Western Hemisphere. But the people at the *Guinness Book of World Records* had another solution: a new category called "Longest bridge over water (continuous)." The entry for this category is, of course, the Lake Pontchartrain Causeway in Louisiana, USA, because if you draw a straight line from the point where the Jiaozhou Bay Bridge starts to where it finishes, eliminating the curves and doubled-backed section to the landmass near the middle, the distance is only about sixteen miles. The Lake Pontchartrain Causeway's direct, point-to-point, entirely over water distance is twenty-four miles. The Jiaozhou Bay Bridge was awarded the record-holding title: "Longest bridge over water (aggregate)."

But you know how pride works. Louisianans do not want to give up any record, whether a new category or an old one. In 2011, Causeway General Manager Carlton Dufrechou said the Causeway can also challenge Jiaozhou's aggregate length claim, as well. In an e-mail to the *Guinness Book of World Records* officials, he wrote, "We understand that all three legs of the bridge [this includes the spans to and from the landmass] were included in the calculation of its cumulative length of 26.4 miles. The Causeway is actually two parallel bridges of 24 miles each with an aggregate length of 48 miles." As a Louisianan, I can say, "We want this record, too!"

But for now, the state will have to be content that the Lake Pontchartrain Causeway will remain an entry in the *Guinness Book of World Records*.

The Causeway continues to provide the best means for those wishing to cross the center of Lake Pontchartrain. Suburbanites travel to work in the bustling city of New Orleans; others are eager to visit the historic French Quarter or uptown Garden District. City folk are headed in the opposite direction. They want to get out of the city and enjoy the amenities on the north shore of the lake. With over thirty thousand vehicles crossing its twin spans every day, the Causeway is predicted to reach full capacity by 2018. Some wild schemes, rivaling the "island" idea of the 1920s, have been proposed, but it seems a third parallel span with safety "shoulders" is already in the planning stage. The middle span would carry traffic to New Orleans in the morning and reverse the traffic out of the city in the evening.

When you call the offices of the Lake Pontchartrain Causeway, you will hear the greeting "Thank you for calling the Causeway, the world's longest bridge."

BIBLIOGRAPHY

And So into the Fray . . . (1827)

Dobie, J. Frank. "Jim Bowie, Big Dealer." *Southwestern Historical Quarterly*, vol. 80, July 1956–April 1957, 342–43.

LaFleur, Jerry. "Bayou Bouef Village, the Bowie Knife and Bunkie, Louisiana." *Bunkie, Louisiana Tattler*, June 2009. www.bunkie .com/BunkieTattler/Archives/bayou_bouef_village.htm. Accessed March 12, 2013.

Whittington, G. P. "Rapides Parish, Louisiana—a History: Second Installment (Continued from October 1932, Quarterly)," *Louisiana Historical Quarterly*, vol. 16, 27–37.

Williamson, William R. "Bowie Knife." *Handbook of Texas Online*. Texas State Historical Association. www.tshaonline.org/handbook/ online/articles/lnb01. Accessed March 12, 2013.

White Sulphur Springs: Healthy or Health Hazard? (1833)

Kingsley, Karen. "Taking the Waters: Louisiana's Early Spas." *Louisiana Cultural Vistas*, vol. 18, no. 3, Fall 2007. New Orleans: Louisiana Endowment for the Humanities. www.nxtbook.com/ nxtbooks/leh/lcv-fall07/index.php?startid=68. Accessed January 15, 2013.

Moorman, J. J. *White Sulphur Springs*. Baltimore: Kelly, Piet & Company, 1869. National Register File at the Louisiana State Historic Preservation Office. Department of Culture, Recreation and Tourism. www.crt.state.la.us/hp/nationalregister/nhl/parish30/ scans/30002001.pdf. Accessed January 10, 2013.

Willis, Jack M. "Sulphur Springs Was Famous Resort." *Piney Woods Journal*, June 2001. www.thepineywoods.com/sulphur.htm. Accessed January 10, 2013.

Breaking Up of the Great Raft (1835)

City of Shreveport. www.caddohistory.com/shreveport_1830s_1860. html. Accessed December 28, 2012.

Fortier, Alcée, ed. *Louisiana: Comprising Sketches of Parishes, Towns, Events, Institutions and Persons, Arranged in Cyclopedic Form*, Vol. 2. Madison, WI: Century Historical Association, 1914. http:// archive.org/stream/louisianacompris02fort#page/n3/mode/2up. pp. 359–60. Accessed December 28, 2012.

Great Raft. www.caddohistory.com/great_raft.html. Accessed December 28, 2012.

Workers of the Writers' Program of the Works Progress Administration in the State of Louisiana, comps. *Louisiana: A Guide to the State.* Baton Rouge: Louisiana State University, 1941, 362–63.

Pecan Trees and Gifted Slave Make History (1846)

Fossett, Judith Jackson. Slavery's Ephemera, "The Contemporary Life of the Antebellum Plantation." *Vectors Journal.* http://vectors.usc .edu/projects/index.php?project=56. Accessed December 13, 2012.

Griffith, Linda, and Fred Griffith. *Nuts: Recipes from around the World That Feature Nature's Perfect Ingredient.* New York: St. Martin's Press, 2003, 27.

Oak Alley Plantation. "About Us." www.Oakalleyplantation.com/ about/history. Accessed December 2, 2012.

Reed, Clarence A. *The Pecan.* U.S. Department of Agriculture, Bureau of Plant Industry, Bulletin No. 251. Washington, DC: Government Printing Office, 1912, 86.

Smith, Andrew F. "The Pecan: A Culinary History." Prepared for the National Pecan Shellers Association Meeting, Charleston, February 21, 2012. http://andrewfsmith.com/wp-content/themes/wooden-mannequin/pdf/PecanHistory.pdf. Accessed December 3, 2012.

Longest Siege in U.S. Civil War History (1863)

Kelly's Confederate Irish Brigade. "Port Hudson." http://kellysconfederateirishbrigade.com/battles.html#LA. Accessed January 15, 2013.

Moneyhon, Carl, and Bobby Roberts. *Portraits of Conflict: A Photographic History of Louisiana in the Civil War.* Fayetteville: University of Arkansas Press, 1990, 191–245.

He Needed Another Miracle (1866)

Goldie, Francis. *The Life of the Blessed John Berchmans.* London: Burns and Oates, Quarterly Series, Volume 7, 1873.

"The Life of St. John Berchmans, S.J." Catholic Pamphlets. www.catholicpamphlets.net/pamphlets/THE%20LIFE%20OF%20ST%20John%20Berchmans.pdf. Accessed February 18, 2013.

McNamara, Dave. "Heart of Louisiana: 'Miracle' at Grand Coteau." *FOX 8, WVUE New Orleans.* www.fox8live.com/story/20047798/heart-of-louisiana-miracle-at-grand-coteau?clienttype=printable. Accessed February 13, 2013.

"Our Saints." *Berchmans Academy of the Sacred Heart.* www.sshcoteau.org/berchmans/prospective-families/saints/. Accessed February 13, 2013.

Twenty-Five Thousand Workers Unite (1892)

Arnesen, Eric, ed. *Encyclopedia of United States Labor and Working-Class History.* New York: Routledge, Taylor & Francis, 2007, 1000–1001.

Cook, Bernard A. "The Typographical Union and the New Orleans General Strike of 1892." *Louisiana History: The Journal of the Louisiana Historical Association*, vol. 24, no. 4, (Autumn 1983), 377–88.

Mahin, Chris. "New Orleans, November 1892: One City's Heroic General Strike Defies Racial Divisions." Education and Mobilization Department of the Chicago & Midwest Regional Joint Board of Unite Here. www.pennfedbmwe.org/?zone=/ unionactive/view_article.cfm&HomeID=95506. Accessed February 15, 2013.

Murfin, Patrick. "The New Orleans Strike of 1892." Working Class Heroes. www.workingclassheroes.me/?p=253. Accessed February 15, 2013.

Man Boards the "Wrong" Railcar (1892)

"Another Jim Crow Car Case. Arrest of a Negro Traveler Who Persisted in Riding with the White People." *Daily Picayune*, July 9, 1892. http://photos.nola.com/tpphotos/2011/09/175plessy_8.html. Accessed January 22, 2013.

Davis, Thomas J. *Plessy v. Ferguson*. Westport, CT: Greenwood Press, 2012.

Woodward, C. Vann. "The Case of the Louisiana Traveler." University of Minnesota, Department of Sociology. www.soc.umn .edu/~samaha/cases/van%20woodward,%20plessy.htm. Accessed January 22, 2013.

The Home That Fear Built (1894)

AcadiaParishToday.com. "Armadillo, Leprosy in Humans Linked." www.acadiaparishtoday.com/pages/full_story/ push?article-Armadillo-+leprosy+in+humans+linked%20 &id=13083819#ixzz2FGK57iXg May 3, 2011. Accessed December 16, 2012.

KnowLa: Encyclopedia of Louisiana. "Carville/National Leprosarium." www.knowla.org/entry.php?rec=576. Accessed December 12, 2012.

Marshall, Darelyn. "History of Iberville Parish U. S. Public Health Service Hospital." www.karensorphans.net/carville.htm. Accessed December 15, 2012.

U.S. Department of Health and Human Services. "History of the National Leprosarium." www.hrsa.gov/hansensdisease/pdfs/hansenshandout3.pdf. Accessed December 12, 2012.

Biggest Auction in Town (1895)

Eunice, Louisiana. www.eunice-la.com. Accessed November 1, 2012.

Fortier, Alcée, ed. *Louisiana: Comprising Sketches of Parishes, Towns, Events, Institutions, and Persons, Arranged in Cyclopedic Form*, Vol. 3, 131–34. Madison, WI: Century Historical Association, 1914. http://archive.org/details/louisianacompris03fort. Accessed January 29, 2013.

Leeper, Clare D'Artois. *Louisiana Place Names.* Baton Rouge: Louisiana State University Press, 2012, 93.

Frogs Ruled the City (1901)

AcadiaParishToday.com. "How Rayne Became Frog Capital." October 7, 2008. www.crowleypostsignal.com/view/full_story/8279328/article-How-Rayne-became-Frog-Capital. Accessed December 6, 2012.

City of Rayne History. www.rayne.org/history.html. Accessed December 6, 2012.

Cramer, John D. "A Look at Rayne, Louisiana." http://johndcramer.wordpress.com/2011/02/18/a-look-at-rayne-louisiana/. Accessed December 6, 2012.

McCarty, Cheryl, and Tony Olinger. *Images of America: Rayne.* Charleston, SC: Arcadia Publishing, 2002, 70–72.

Valdman, Albert, ed. *Dictionary of Louisiana French*. Jackson: The University Press of Mississippi, 2010, 430.

Heywood's Heyday (1901)

Bradshaw, Jim. "Louisiana Industry Began on Jules Clément." *Lafayette (LA) Daily Advertiser*, October 28, 1997. www.carencrohighschool .org/LA_Studies/ParishSeries/JeffersonDavisParish/OilIndustry.htm. Accessed March 3, 2013.

Riser, Henry LeRoy. "The History of Jennings, Louisiana." Louisiana State University and Agricultural and Mechanical College thesis, August 1948. http://library.mcneese.edu/depts/archive/FTBooks/ jennings.htm. Accessed March 9, 2013.

State of Louisiana. History of Oil & Gas in Louisiana and the Gulf Coast Region. http://dnr.louisiana.gov/assets/TAD/education/ BGBB/6/la_oil.html. Accessed March 3, 2013.

Jungle Man Comes to Town (1917)

Besson, Eric. *Gumbo Entertainment Guide*. "Nearly 95 Years Later, Tarzan Returns." April 3, 2012. www.tri-parishtimes.com/gumbo/ article_fbd92d36-7dbb-11e1-ab4b-001a4bcf887a.html. Accessed October 12, 2012.

ERBzine. www.erbzine.com/mag31/3110.html. Accessed October 12, 2012.

Laney, Ruth. "Tracking Down Tarzan." *Country Roads*. March 2012.

Boll Weevils Build an Airline (1922)

Century of Flight. "Airlines and Airliners." www.century-of-flight.net/ Aviation%20history/coming%20of%20age/usairlines/Delta%20 Airlines.htm. Accessed June 25, 2012.

Cleveland, T. C., and C. R. Parencia. "History of the USDA Cotton Insects Research Laboratory Tallulah, Louisiana, 1909–1973." *Bulletin of the Entomological Society of America*, vol. 22, no. 4, December 1976, 403–407.

Delta Heritage Museum. "Delta History." http://deltamuseum.org/M_Education_DeltaHistory_Facts_History.htm. Accessed January 5, 2013.

Harper, Timothy. "Crop-Dusters Were the Beginning of a Great Airline in the 1920s." *Delta's Sky Magazine*. Minneapolis, MN: MSP Communications, March 2004.

Lecky, C. S., and Minnie S. Murphy. "History of Tallulah Laboratory, Bureau of Entomology, U.S. Department of Agriculture." Work Project Administration (WPA) Project, June 3, 1936. www.rootsweb.ancestry.com/~lamadiso/articles/bughistory.htm. Accessed January 1, 2013.

Martin, John Earl. "A History of Ag Aviation in Madison Parish, Tallulah, Louisiana." October 2004. www.rootsweb.ancestry.com/~lamadiso/articles/agaviation.htm. Accessed January 6, 2013.

Workman, Noel. "The Birth of an Airline in a Delta Cotton Field." *Delta's Sky Magazine*. Minneapolis, MN: MSP Communications, September/October 2011. www.deltamagazine.com/delta.html. Accessed June 25, 2012.

Canadian Husky Finds Eternal Rest in Louisiana Soil (1931)

Find a Grave. "Unalaska Byrd." www.findagrave.com/cgi-bin/fg.cgi?page=gr&GRid=33344880. Accessed December 12, 2012.

WNOE.com. "Did You Know? Georgia and Unalaska." November 1, 2012. www.knoe.com/story/13425514/did-you-know-. Accessed December 13, 2012.

BIBLIOGRAPHY

Playing for the Championship (1932)

Aiello, Thomas. *Bayou Classic: The Grambling-Southern Football Rivalry.* Baton Rouge: Louisiana State University Press, 2010, 19.

———. "The Composition of Kings." *Baseball Research Journal.* Phoenix, AZ: Society for American Baseball Research, Vol. 35, 2006, 1–14.

———. *The Kings of Casino Park: Black Baseball in the Lost Season of 1932.* Tuscaloosa: University of Alabama Press, 2011, 79.

Fergus, Preston. AAPGDatapages/Archives. AAPG Special Volumes. http://archives.datapages.com/data/specpubs/fieldst1/data/a004/ a004/0001/0700/0741.htm. Accessed December 12, 2012.

They Got What They Had Coming (1934)

Henry Methvin. Methvin Online. www.tmethvin.com/henry/. Accessed October 10, 2012.

Steele, Phillip W., and Marie Barrow Scoma. *The Family Story of Bonnie and Clyde.* Gretna, LA: Pelican Publishing Company, 2003.

Stuart, Bonnye. *Louisiana Curiosities.* Guilford, CT: Globe Pequot, 2012.

The King Is Dead (1935)

Long Legacy Project. "Assassination." www.hueylong.com/life-times/ assassination.php. Accessed December 13, 2012.

Watkins, Thayer. "Huey Long: His Life and Times." San Jose State University, Department of Economics. www.sjsu.edu/faculty/ watkins/hlong.htm. Accessed February 15, 2013.

Bombing with Sacks of Flour (1941)

Perry, Mark. "Louisiana Maneuvers (1940–41)." *Historynet.com.* www .historynet.com/louisiana-maneuvers-1940-41.htm. Accessed April 20, 2013.

"Stories of the Great Louisiana Maneuvers." *Treasurenet.* www
.treasurenet.com/forums/louisiana/67933-stories-great-louisiana-
maneuvers.html. Accessed April 20, 2013.

Vernon Parish Tourism Commission. "The Great Louisiana
Maneuvers." www.venturevernon.com/ManeuversMOB.html.
Accessed April 18, 2013.

Famous P.O.W. Gets a Taste of Louisiana (1942)

"Camp Livingston (Louisiana) USA POW Camp." *World and Military
Notes.com.* http://worldandmilitarynotes.com/pow/camp-livingston-
louisiana-usa-pow-camp/. Accessed March 22, 2013.

Densho Encyclopedia. "Camp Livingston (detention facility)." http://
encyclopedia.densho.org/Camp_Livingston%20(detention%20
facility)/. Accessed March 22, 2013.

German American Internee Coalition. http://gaic.info/Images/
Inouye%20memoirs.pdf Accessed March 22, 2013.

Prisoner of War Camp. http://camp-livingston.winnfreenet.com/pow
.php. Accessed March 19, 2013.

Sakamaki, Kazuo. *I Attacked Pearl Harbor.* New York: Association
Press, 1949.

Sanson, Jerry Purvis. *Louisiana during World War II.* Baton Rouge:
Louisiana State University Press, 1999, 195–205.

Dead Woman Walking (1942)

Gillespie, Kay. *Executed Women of 20th and 21st Centuries.* New York:
University Press of America, 2009, 46.

O'Shea, Kathleen. *Women and Death Penalty in the United States:
1900–1998.* Westport, CT: Praeger Publishers, 1999, 92.

"Toni Jo Henry, a Love Worth Dying For?" www
.capitalpunishmentuk.org/tonijo.html. Accessed March 15, 2013.

Heel String Gang Makes Their Demands Heard (1951)

Churcher, Kalen Mary Ann. "Self-Governance, Normalcy and Control: Inmate-Produced Media at the Louisiana State Penitentiary at Angola." PhD dissertation, mass communications, Pennsylvania State University, 2008.

McShane, Marilyn D., and Franklin P. Williams III, eds. "Prison Life in the 1950s. American Decades. 2001." *Encyclopedia of American Prisons.* New York: Taylor & Francis, 2005, 53–54. http://roohit .com/b99b3. Accessed March 14, 2015.

Staff Correspondent. "Self-Mutilation Outbreak in U.S. Prison." *Sydney Morning Herald,* February 28, 1951, 3. http://news.google .com/newspapers?nid=1301&dat=19510228&id=6fxUAAAAIBAJ &sjid=JJMDAAAAIBAJ&pg=3589,3955895. Accessed March 20, 2013.

Stagg, Edward W., and John Lear. "America's Worst Prison." *Collier's Weekly,* vol. 130 (November 22, 1952): 13–16.

Wilson, Donald Powell, and Harry Elmer Barnes. "A Riot Is an Unnecessary Evil." *Life Magazine,* November 24, 1952, 138–50.

Louisiana Hayride Jump Starts a Career (1954)

Donaldson, Elvalee. "The Rocket Who Rocks n Rolls." *Lakeland Ledger.* August 2, 1956. www.elvisconcerts.com/newspapers/ press315.htm. Accessed February 18, 2013.

Laird, Tracey. *Louisiana Hayride: Radio and Roots Music along the Red River.* New York: Oxford University Press, 2005.

Run, Billy, Run! (1959)

Guilbeau, Glenn. "LSU Legend Billy Canon in Intensive Care after Stroke." *USA Today* Sports, February 20, 2013.

Longman, Jere. "Never Forgotten, Billy Cannon Is Now Forgiven."
New York Times, College Football, December 28, 2003. www
.nytimes.com/2003/12/28/sports/college-football-never-forgotten-
billy-cannon-is-now-forgiven.html?pagewanted=all&src=pm.
Accessed March 13, 2013.

Rudeen, Kenneth. "Tiger on the Prowl." *Sports Illustrated*, November
9, 1959.

Thompson, Wright. "The Redemption of Billy Cannon." *ESPN:*
Outside the Lines. http://sports.espn.go.com/espn/eticket/
story?page=091030BillyCannon. Accessed March 12, 2013.

Woodstock Festival in Rural Louisiana? Not! (1971)

Campbell, Rick. "40 Years After: Historical Pop Culture with Rick
Campbell." *Houston Chronicle*, June 27, 2011. http://blog.chron
.com/40yearsafter/2011/06/celebrating-life-the-hard-way/. Accessed
March 8, 2013.

"The Louisiana Festival: Sellabration of Life." *Ann Arbor Sun*, July 9,
1971. http://oldnews.aadl.org/node/193657. Accessed March 8,
2013.

Parting Shots. "Perhaps the Last of the Rock Festival Fiascos." *Life*
Magazine, July 9, 1971, 72.

Santelli, Robert. "This Ain't the Summer of Love." http://
thisaintthesummeroflove.blogspot.com/2011/06/40-years-ago-this-
week-june-21-28-1971.html. Accessed March 8, 2013.

United Press International (UPI). "'Celebration of Life' Rockfest
Halted." *Sarasota Herald-Tribune*, June 20, 1971, 2-A. http://news
.google.com/newspapers?nid=1755&dat=19710620&id=Bz0gA
AAAIBAJ&sjid=fGYEAAAAIBAJ&pg=5275,1180338. Accessed
March 8, 2013.

The Case of the Disappearing Freshwater Lake (1980)

"And Away Goes the Lake down the Drain." Lake Peigneur. http://
web.archive.org/web/20071230013705/http://members.tripod
.com/~earthdude1/texaco/texaco.html. Accessed March 22, 2013.

"Barges Pop Up Like Corks in Lake." *Tuscaloosa News*, Sunday,
November 12, 1980, 3A. http://news.google.com/newspapers?nid=
1817&dat=19801123&id=hAgdAAAAIBAJ&sjid=1J4EAAAAIBAJ
&pg=4299,5555671. Accessed March 22, 2013.

Bellows, Allen. "Lake Peigneur: The Swirling Vortex of Doom, New
Iberia, Louisiana." Endangered Earth: Sinkholes Assorted. www
.thelivingmoon.com/45jack_files/03files/Endangered_Earth_
Sinkhole_Louisiana.html. Accessed March 24, 2013.

"Lake Peigneur." http://home.versatel.nl/the_sims/rig/lakepeigneur
.htm. Accessed March 22, 2013.

Thousands Seek the Virgin Mary (1989)

American Folklore Society. "Our Lady of Tickfaw Records, 1995."
www.folklorecollections.org/index.php/Detail/Object/Show/object_
id/51. Accessed March 14, 2015.

Ashton, Linda. "Some Claim Religious Visions as Thousands Visit
Tiny La. Town." AP Archive. March 12, 1989. www.apnewsarchive
.com/1989/Hundreds-Looking-for-Apparition-of-Virgin-Mary/
id-9f8ebebbcb98d5637904fc020a4cdaf0. Accessed January 21,
2013.

Associated Press. "Hundreds Looking for Apparition of Virgin
Mary." AP Archive. Mar. 11, 1989. www.apnewsarchive
.com/1989/Hundreds-Looking-for-Apparition-of-Virgin-Mary/id-
9f8ebebbcb98d5637904fc020a4cdaf0. Accessed January 21, 2013.

Stuart, Bonnye. *Louisiana Curiosities*. Guilford, CT: Globe Pequot
Press, 2012.

Mardi Gras Shipwreck Celebrates History Underwater (2007)

Hall, Andy. "Mardi Gras Wreck: U.S. Privateer *Rapid*?" Maritime Texas. http://maritimetexas.net/wordpress/?p=802. Accessed April 22, 2013.

McNamara, Dave. "Heart of Louisiana: The Mardi Gras shipwreck." *Fox8Live*. www.fox8live.com/story/19897797/heart-of-louisiana. Accessed April 20, 2013.

Pope, John. "Mysterious Shipwreck Unearthed at Bottom Gulf." *Times-Picayune*, March 8, 2009. CNN iReport. http://ireport.cnn .com/docs/DOC-226863. Accessed April 22, 2013.

More than Just an Oily Mess (2010)

"BP Oil Spill Clean-Up to Cost Nearly $5 Billion." *Environmental Leader: Environmental & Energy Management News*, May 3, 2010. www.environmentalleader.com/2010/05/03/bp-oil-spill-clean-up-to-cost-nearly-5-billion/. Accessed April 6, 2013.

"Eyeless Shrimp and Mutant Fish Raise Concerns over BP Spill Effects." FoxNews.com, April 18, 2012. www.foxnews.com/ scitech/2012/04/18/eyeless-shrimp-and-mutant-fish-raise-concerns-over-bp-spill-effects/#ixzz2PoaVC0cG. Accessed April 6, 2013.

Jamail, Dahr. "Gulf Seafood Deformities Alarm Scientists." *Al Jazeera English*, Features. www.aljazeera.com/indepth/ features/2012/04/201241682318260912.html. Accessed April 7, 2013.

Kirkham, Chris. "Rescued Oil Rig Explosion Workers Arrive to Meet Families at Kenner Hotel." *Times-Picayune*, April 29, 2010. www .nola.com/news/index.ssf/2010/04/rescued_oil_rig_workers_arrive .html. Accessed April 6, 2013.

Tangley, Laura. "The American Bird Conservancy Releases List of Top 10 Sites at Most Immediate Risk from Deepwater Horizon Oil Spill." *National Wildlife*, June 17, 2010. www.nwf.org/News-and-Magazines/National-Wildlife/Birds/Archives/2010/Oil-Spill-Birds .aspx. Accessed April 6, 2013.

Weber, Harry R. "Blown-Out BP Well Finally Killed at Bottom of Gulf." *Boston Globe*, September 19, 2010. www.boston.com/news/ nation/articles/2010/09/19/blown_out_bp_well_finally_killed_at_ bottom_of_gulf/. Accessed April 6, 2013.

Week's Editorial Staff. "BP Oil Spill: The 'Horribly Mutated' Creatures Living in the Gulf." *Yahoo News*, April 19, 2012. http:// news.yahoo.com/bp-oil-spill-horribly-mutated-creatures-living-gulf-180100880.html. Accessed April 6, 2013.

Still Making the *Guinness Book of World Records* (2011)

AA Roads. "Lake Pontchartrain Causeway." www.southeastroads.com/ pc.html. Accessed March 31, 2013.

Warren, Bob. "Guinness World Records Opens New Category for Lake Pontchartrain Causeway." *Times-Picayune*. www.nola.com/ traffic/index.ssf/2011/07/guinness_world_records_opens_n.html. Accessed March 31, 2013.

INDEX

INDEX

ABOUT THE AUTHOR

Bonnye Stuart is a ninth-generation New Orleans, Louisiana, native. She got her BA in advertising from the Manship School of Journalism at Louisiana State University and received her MA in communication from the University of New Orleans. She has been teaching at the university level for twenty-six years and at Winthrop University for fourteen years. She teaches public relations, corporate communication, and international communication in the Department of Mass Communication. Before teaching she worked as a public relations professional for both for-profit and nonprofit organizations. She has had short stories, poems, and historically based stories and biographies published and has had several plays produced. Stuart is the author of *It Happened In New Orleans, More Than Petticoats: Remarkable Louisiana Women, Louisiana Curiosities, Discovering Vintage New Orleans,* and *Haunted New Orleans* (all Globe Pequot). She enjoys travel and viewing the world from various global perspectives. She has interviewed PR professionals in France, England, Greece, Thailand, and Singapore. Her research interests focus on the power of media images, specifically their early influence on the Troubles of Northern Ireland and their role as agent for social change. She is married to Laurence P. Stuart, and they have four married children and ten grandchildren.